KÖNEMANN

© 2015 for this edition: koenemann.com GmbH
Distributed in cooperation with Frechmann Kolón GmbH

www.koenemann.com
www.frechmann.com

Published in the United States in 2016 by:

Skyhorse Publishing
307 West 36th Street, 11th Floor
New York, NY 10018, USA
T: +1 212 643 6816

info@skyhorsepublishing.com
www.skyhorsepublishing.com

Editorial project: LOFT Publications
Barcelona, Spain
Tel.: +34 932 688 088
Fax: +34 932 687 073
loft@loftpublications.com
www.loftpublications.com

Editorial coordinator: Simone K. Schleifer
Assistant to editorial coordination: Aitana Lleonart
Editor and Texts: Marta Serrats
Art director: Mireia Casanovas Soley
Design and layout coordination: Claudia Martínez Alonso
Layout: Anabel N. Quintana
Translations: Equipo de Edición

ISBN 978-3-86407-202-4 (GB)
ISBN 978-3-86407-200-0 (D)
ISBN 978-3-86407-201-7 (E)
ISBN 978-1-5107-0452-7 (Skyhorse, USA)

Printed in Spain

Introduction / Introduction

Art, agriculture and ecology are the three defining elements around which contemporary exterior-design trends are revolving. In reality, it does not respond to a new breakthrough trend but rather the traditional concept of creating and maintaining landscaped spaces and making them compatible with other current forms of understanding gardening. Green spaces have gone from being just an aesthetic contribution to the landscape to a key element in sustainable and environmental development.

This book offers different exterior spaces classified by type: terraces, balconies, patios and roofgardens; projects articulated around the work areas that comprise the most representative trends of the modern garden. The currency of the different designs lies in this new form of landscape gardening called "agritecture", a harmonious symbiosis between construction, living environment and human activity. The latter becomes a determinant factor in designing an exterior space adapted to each person's requirements. Frenetic urbanism has converted green spaces, particularly ones that form part of a home, into places in which to unwind. The benefits extend beyond those of a solitary garden. Their presence in intermediate spaces makes them a micro-cosmos that helps improve city dwellers' quality of life. Lack of space, lack of fertile soil, lack of time and lack of light usually characterize these gardens that are difficult to resolve. But modern building techniques, materials and equipment have without a doubt made them an inhabitable piece more in keeping with a property's other rooms.

Moreover, respect for the environment and use of available natural resources have slowly become a priority for guaranteeing the sustainability of landscaped spaces. Water reuse is key to attaining an ecological balance. Examples can be found in a number of the projects presented here, with the creation of pools or water features that use rainwater to nurture the garden.

The search for a return to nature leads to the creation of exterior spaces closely related to free and exuberant vegetation. The idea is to create a feeling of an indomitable space, with flora that emerges directly from the natural environment and using trees that could form part of a wild rainforest. In this regard, some of the examples presented here seek to mimic the environment, attempting to emulate the surrounding autochthonous landscape.

The strategies used by the designers and architects featured in the book highlight the resources for incorporating a garden into our habitat to offset daily life dominated by asphalt and lacking in public green spaces. Conserving periurban natural spaces and boosting urban green zones should be priorities in future urban-planning approaches toward our cities, and essential aspects in improving the urban landscape and quality of life of citizens.

L'art, l'agriculture et l'écologie sont les trois axes autour desquels s'organisent les nouvelles tendances du « vivre dehors » en vogue aujourd'hui. Il ne s'agit pas, en réalité, d'un nouveau courant, mais du concept traditionnel de création et d'entretien d'espaces verts qu'il faut rendre compatible avec les façons actuelles de penser le jardinage. Les espaces verts ne sont plus uniquement une contribution esthétique au paysage et sont devenus un élément clé dans le développement durable et la gestion de l'environnement.

Ce livre présente différents espaces extérieurs, classés par typologie : terrasses, balcons, cours et toits-jardins ; des projets qui s'articulent autour des lignes d'action formant les tendances les plus représentatives du jardin moderne, notamment celle que l'on appelle « agritecture », une symbiose entre construction, environnement vivant et activité humaine. C'est cette dernière qui devient un facteur déterminant dans la projection d'un espace extérieur adapté aux besoins de chacun. La frénésie urbaine a transformé les espaces verts, surtout ceux faisant partie de la maison, en zones de détente. Leurs avantages vont au-delà de ceux d'un jardin isolé. Leur présence dans des espaces intermédiaires en fait un microcosme qui contribue à améliorer la qualité de vie des habitants de la ville. Le manque d'espace, de sol fertile, de temps, de lumière caractérisent généralement ces jardins difficiles à concevoir. Cependant, les techniques actuelles de construction, les matériaux et l'équipement les ont transformés sans aucun doute en un nouvel espace à vivre accolé aux autres pièces de la maison.

D'un autre côté, le respect de l'environnement et l'exploitation des ressources naturelles disponibles sont devenus progressivement une priorité pour garantir la durabilité de l'espace vert. La réutilisation de l'eau est la clé pour atteindre l'équilibre écologique. Certains des projets présentés ici en sont un exemple, avec la création d'étangs ou d'autres espaces humides permettant d'utiliser l'eau de pluie pour arroser le jardin.

Le retour à la nature conduit à élaborer des espaces extérieurs très proches de ce qu'est la végétation libre et exubérante. On essaye de créer un lieu indompté, avec une flore provenant directement du milieu naturel, en utilisant des arbres qui pourraient faire partie d'une forêt sauvage. Ainsi, certains exemples présentés dans les pages qui suivent recherchent un mimétisme avec l'environnement autochtone.

Les stratégies utilisées par les designers et les architectes rassemblées dans ce livre mettent l'accent sur les ressources permettant d'intégrer le jardin à notre habitat et de compenser ainsi un quotidien dominé par l'asphalte et souvent dépourvu d'espaces verts publics. Conserver les espaces naturels périurbains ou augmenter les zones vertes urbaines devrait constituer une priorité dans les approches urbanistiques futures de nos villes et un aspect essentiel pour l'amélioration du paysage urbain et la qualité de vie des citoyens.

Einleitung / Inleiding

Kunst, Architektur und Umwelt – dies sind die Eckpunkte, an denen die neuesten Tendenzen bei der Begrünung von Außenanlagen festgemacht werden können. Dabei handelt es sich eigentlich nicht um eine ganz neue Entwicklung: Wie seit jeher geht es darum, Grünräume anzulegen und zu erhalten, nun allerdings im heutigen Verständnis von Garten- und Landschaftsbau. Grünanlagen werden nicht mehr nur als ein ästhetischer Beitrag gesehen: Sie sind integraler Bestandteil umweltverträglicher Planung.

Dieses Buch stellt begrünte Außenräume verschiedener Art vor: Terrassen, Balkone, Höfe und begrünte Dächer. Alle ausgewählten Projekte stehen repräsentativ für die vorherrschenden Gestaltungstendenzen im modernen Gartenbau. Charakteristisch für diese zeitgenössischen Vorschläge ist eine neue Auffassung bei Gestaltung von Außenanlagen, die auch als Agritecture bekannt ist. Dabei handelt es sich um eine Symbiose aus Bauen, lebendiger Umwelt und menschlicher Tätigkeit. Eben diese menschliche Aktivität ist der ausschlaggebende Faktor beim Entwurf von Außenbereichen, die den Bedürfnissen der jeweiligen Bauherrn angepasst sind. Die Hektik in den Städten hat Grünräume, besonders jene, die direkt zum Wohnbereich gehören, zu Orten gewollter Langsamkeit werden lassen. Die Vorzüge eines abgeschlossenen Privatgartens auf individueller Ebene verbinden sich hier mit einem positiven Einfluss auf die Verbesserung des Mikroklimas, das die Lebensqualität aller Stadtbewohner verbessert. Die Begrenztheit des zur Verfügung stehenden Raums, der Mangel an fruchtbarem Boden und oftmals das Fehlen einer natürlichen Beleuchtung stellen die größten Probleme bei der Anlage eines solchen urbanen Gartens dar. Und doch ermöglicht die moderne Bautechnik den Einsatz von Materialien und technischen Hilfsmitteln, die aus einer solchen Grünanlage einen Aufenthaltsraum machen, der zu einem unverzichtbaren Bestandteil der Wohnung wird.

Zugleich sind Umweltverträglichkeit und optimale, nachhaltige Nutzung der verfügbaren natürlichen Ressourcen in letzter Zeit zu Prioritäten im Gartenbau geworden. So ist der sparsame Umgang mit dem Wasser kennzeichnend für umweltverträgliches Bauen. Bei einigen der vorgestellten Projekte wird das anfallende Regenwasser für die Bewässerung von Teichen und Feuchtbiotopen genutzt.

Auf dem Weg zurück zur Natur entstehen Außenräume, in denen das ungehinderte Wachstum üppiger Pflanzen bewusst gefördert wird. So soll der Eindruck eines unberührten Ortes hervorgerufen werden, an dem Pflanzen aus der Natur der näheren Umgebung wachsen, Bäume, wie sie auch in jedem wild wachsenden Wald zu finden sind. Daher hat man sich bei manchen der ausgewählten Entwürfe bemüht, Naturräume neu zu schaffen, die der Landschaft der Umgebung nachempfunden sind.

In den Entwürfen der Landschaftsarchitekten und Gartengestalter, die hier zu sehen sind, wird deutlich, welche Strategien jeweils angewandt und welche Mittel eingesetzt wurden, um den Garten zu einem Teil der Wohnung zu machen und auf diese Weise der Dominanz von Asphalt und Beton im Alltag etwas entgegenzusetzen. Die Erhaltung stadtnaher Naturräume und die Schaffung neuer innerstädtischer Grünflächen sollte eine Priorität bei der Stadtplanung der Zukunft darstellen, um die Stadtlandschaft zu verbessern und die Lebensqualität der Stadtbewohner zu erhöhen.

De huidige trends in de tuinarchitectuur draaien om kunst, landbouw en ecologie. In feite gaat het niet om stromingen die breken met het oude, maar om stijlen waarin de traditionele ideeën over tuinaanleg en onderhoud worden gecombineerd met andere, hedendaagse denkwijzen over tuinieren. Groene ruimten dragen niet langer uitsluitend in esthetische zin bij aan het landschap, maar zijn een belangrijk element geworden in een algemene ontwikkeling in de richting van duurzaamheid en milieubewustzijn.

Dit boek biedt een overzicht van buitenruimten die zijn ingedeeld naar hun functie: terrassen, balkons, patio's en daktuinen. De ontwerpen ervan zijn vormgegeven volgens de laatste trends in de tuinarchitectuur. Het moderne karakter van de diverse ontwerpen zit in de interpretatie van wat de laatste tendensen op het gebied van tuinarchitectuur, de zogeheten *agritectuur*, zijn. Het gaat hoe dan ook om een harmonieuze combinatie van constructie, levende omgeving en menselijke activiteit. De laatste is de bepalende factor bij ontwerpen van een buitenruimte die rekening houden met alle drie. In het gejaagde stadsleven zijn groene ruimten plaatsen van rust geworden, vooral de ruimten die bij een woning horen. De eigen tuin heeft nog meer waarde dan openbare tuinen. Hun aanwezigheid in overgangsgebied maakt ze tot microkosmossen die de kwaliteit van het leven van de bewoners verbeteren. Het gebrek aan ruimte, aan vruchtbare grond, aan tijd en licht zijn de uitdagingen die bepalend zijn voor deze tuinen. Dankzij moderne bouwmethoden, materialen en voorzieningen zijn ze tot een verlengstuk van de woonruimte geworden.

Tegelijkertijd zijn respect voor de omgeving en het gebruik van natuurlijke hulpbronnen een prioriteit geworden die de duurzaamheid van de tuinruimte moet waarborgen. Het hergebruik van water is de sleutel tot ecologisch evenwicht. Voorbeelden daarvan zijn te vinden in de hierna getoonde ontwerpen, waarvoor vijvers of andere reservoirs zijn gecreëerd om regenwater op te vangen voor besproeiing.

De zoektocht naar natuurlijker oplossingen resulteert in buitenruimten die qua aanzien dicht bij wilde tuinen liggen waarin de vegetatie vrij lijkt te woekeren. Daarbij wordt gepoogd een gevoel van ongetemdheid te creëren, met planten die uit de natuurlijke omgeving afkomstig zijn en bomen die uit een wild bos zouden kunnen komen. In enkele voorbeelden in dit boek is goed te zien hoe geprobeerd is de omgeving na te bootsen teneinde de inheemse natuur te evenaren.

De door de ontwerpers en architecten gebruikte strategieën die in dit boek gebundeld zijn, laten zien met welke middelen de tuin aan de menselijke habitat is toegevoegd en hoe de alledaagse aanblik van het dominerende asfalt, dat zo slecht past bij de openbare groene ruimte, wordt gecompenseerd. Het behoud van de natuurlijke ruimte aan de stadsrand en het groener maken van de stad zelf zouden prioriteiten in de ontwikkelingsplannen van steden en essentiële aspecten voor de verbetering van het stedelijke landschap en de kwaliteit van leven van de stedelingen moeten zijn.

Introducción / Introduzione

Arte, agricultura y ecología son los tres ejes en torno a los que giran las nuevas tendencias del exteriorismo actual. En realidad, no se trata de una nueva corriente rupturista. Se trata del concepto tradicional de crear y mantener espacios ajardinados, y hacerlo compatible con otros modos actuales de entender la jardinería. Los espacios verdes han pasado de ser únicamente una contribución estética al paisaje a convertirse en un elemento clave en el desarrollo sostenible y medioambiental.

El libro ofrece diferentes espacios exteriores clasificados según su tipología: terrazas, balcones, patios y cubiertas ajardinadas; proyectos que se articulan en torno a las líneas de actuación que conforman las tendencias más representativas del jardín moderno. La contemporaneidad de las diferentes propuestas radica en esta nueva forma de hacer exteriorismo, la denominada agritectura, una armónica simbiosis entre construcción, entorno vivo y actividad humana. Es esta última la que se convierte en un factor determinante a la hora de proyectar un espacio exterior adaptado a las necesidades de cada uno. El frenesí urbano ha convertido los espacios verdes, sobre todo los que forman parte de la vivienda, en puntos de desaceleración. Sus beneficios van más allá de los propios de un jardín aislado. Su presencia en espacios intermedios lo convierte en un microcosmos que ayuda a mejorar la calidad de vida de los habitantes de la urbe. La falta de espacio, de suelo fértil, de tiempo y de luz que suelen caracterizar estos jardines son difíciles de resolver. Sin embargo, las actuales técnicas constructivas, los materiales y el equipamiento lo han convertido, sin lugar a dudas, en una pieza habitable más junto con el resto de estancias de la vivienda.

Por otro lado, el respeto al entorno y el aprovechamiento de los recursos naturales disponibles se han convertido poco a poco en una prioridad para garantizar la sostenibilidad del espacio ajardinado. La reutilización del agua es la clave para alcanzar el equilibrio ecológico. Es el caso de alguno de los proyectos que se presentan a continuación, con la creación de estanques o humedades para aprovechar el agua de la lluvia en el riego del jardín.

La búsqueda del retorno a la naturaleza lleva a la realización de espacios exteriores muy próximos a lo que es la vegetación libre y exuberante. Se intenta crear una sensación de lugar indómito, con flora procedente directamente del medio natural y usando árboles que podrían formar parte de un bosque salvaje. En este sentido, algunos de los ejemplos aquí presentados buscan el mimetismo con el entorno intentando emular el paisaje autóctono que los rodea.

Las estrategias utilizadas por los diseñadores y arquitectos que recopila este libro ponen de manifiesto los recursos para incorporar el jardín a nuestro hábitat y, de este modo, compensar la cotidianidad dominada por el asfalto, que anda coja de espacios verdes públicos. Conservar los espacios naturales periurbanos o potenciar las zonas verdes urbanas debería ser una prioridad en los planteamientos urbanísticos futuros de nuestras ciudades, y un aspecto esencial para la mejora del paisaje urbano y la calidad de vida de los ciudadanos.

L'arte, l'agricoltura e l'ecologia sono i tre cardini intorno ai quali si muovono le attuali tendenze del design d'esterni. Non si tratta, in realtà, di una nuova corrente di rottura, quanto piuttosto di assumere il concetto tradizionale, consistente nel creare e conservare spazi verdi, e renderlo compatibile con altre modalità contemporanee d'intendere il giardinaggio. Dall'essere un mero contributo estetico al paesaggio, le aree verdi sono divenute un elemento fondamentale nello sviluppo sostenibile e rispettoso dell'ambiente.

Questo libro offre diversi esempi di spazi esterni classificati in base alla loro tipologia: terrazze, balconi, cortili e giardini pensili, progetti articolati in funzione delle linee operative che costituiscono le tendenze maggiormente rappresentative del giardino moderno. La contemporaneità delle varie proposte ha le sue radici in una nuova forma di concepire e realizzare il design d'esterni, la cosiddetta agritettura, un'armonica simbiosi tra costruzione, ambiente vivo e attività umana. È proprio quest'ultima a convertirsi in un fattore determinante, quando si tratta di progettare uno spazio esterno adatto alle necessità delle singole persone. La frenesia delle città ha trasformato le aree verdi, soprattutto quelle che fanno parte dell'edilizia abitativa, in punti di decelerazione, ma i loro benefici superano di molto quelli di un giardino isolato, la cui presenza in spazi intermedi è un microcosmo che contribuisce a migliorare la qualità della vita degli abitanti urbani. L'assenza di spazio, la mancanza di suolo fertile, la scarsità di tempo e di luce che caratterizzano di solito questi giardini sono problemi di difficile soluzione. Le attuali tecniche edili, tuttavia, i materiali e le attrezzature sono riusciti a trasformarlo, senza dubbio, in un altro elemento abitabile accanto al resto di stanze di un'abitazione.

D'altro canto, il rispetto per l'ambiente e lo sfruttamento delle risorse naturali disponibili sono diventati lentamente un bisogno prioritario per garantire la sostenibilità dello spazio con giardino. Il riutilizzo dell'acqua è la chiave per raggiungere l'equilibrio ecologico; alcuni progetti presentati qui ne sono un chiaro esempio, con la creazione di bacini che servono per irrigare il giardino utilizzando l'acqua della pioggia.

La ricerca del ritorno alla natura conduce alla realizzazione di spazi esterni molto simili alla vegetazione libera e rigogliosa. Si cerca di creare una sensazione di luogo indomito, con flora direttamente proveniente dal contesto naturale locale e usando alberi che potrebbero trovarsi in un bosco selvatico. In tal senso, alcuni degli esempi che presentiamo in questa sede, tendono al mimetismo con l'ambiente o, in altri termini, a emulare il paesaggio autoctono che li circonda.

Le strategie utilizzate dai designer e dagli architetti raccolti in questo libro fanno emergere le risorse che si possono utilizzare per incorporare il giardino nel nostro habitat e, così facendo, compensare una quotidianità dominata dall'asfalto, in cui scarseggiano gli spazi verdi pubblici. Conservare gli spazi naturali periurbani o aumentare le zone verdi urbane dovrebbe essere una priorità nei futuri piani regolatori delle nostre città, ma anche un aspetto essenziale per il miglioramento del paesaggio urbano e della qualità della vita dei cittadini.

Introdução / Introduktion

Arte, agricultura e ecologia são os três eixos em torno dos quais giram as novas tendências para a decoração de exteriores. Na realidade, não se trata de uma nova corrente de ruptura, e sim de adaptar o conceito tradicional de criar e manter espaços ajardinados a princípios a que a jardinagem deve obedecer nos nossos dias. Os espaços verdes deixaram de restringir-se a uma função meramente estética para se converterem num elemento determinante para o desenvolvimento sustentável do meio ambiente.

Este livro expõe diferentes espaços exteriores classificados segundo uma tipologia própria: terraços, varandas, pátios e coberturas ajardinadas; projectos que se articulam em torno de linhas de actuação que respeitam as tendências mais representativas do jardim moderno. A contemporaneidade das diferentes propostas baseia-se nesta nova forma de configurar o exterior, a denominada *agritectura,* uma simbiose harmónica entre construção, meio ambiente e actividade humana. É esta última que se revela um factor determinante no projecto de um espaço exterior direccionado para a satisfação dos requisitos individuais. O frenesim urbano converteu os espaços verdes, sobretudo os que fazem parte de residências, em marcos de desaceleração. Os benefícios que se colhem transcendem os inerentes ao jardim em si. A sua presença em zonas de passagem representa um microcosmos que contribui significativamente para a melhoria da qualidade de vida dos habitantes da cidade. A falta de espaço, a falta de solo fértil, a falta de tempo e a falta de luminosidade costumam ser as condicionantes mais difíceis de resolver e controlar. Apesar disso, as actuais técnicas de construção, os materiais e os equipamentos transformam o jardim, sem sombra de dúvida, numa peça tão habitável como os restantes compartimentos da residência.

Paralelamente, o respeito pelo ambiente e o aproveitamento de recursos naturais disponíveis converteram-se, pouco a pouco, numa prioridade para garantir a sustentabilidade do espaço ajardinado. A reutilização da água é o segredo para alcançar o equilíbrio ecológico. Alguns dos projectos em curso são já exemplo de aplicação das medidas necessárias, criando tanques ou humidades para aproveitar a água da chuva na rega do jardim.

A procura do retorno à natureza leva à configuração de espaços exteriores à imagem de uma vegetação natural e exuberante. O objectivo é criar uma sensação de lugar indómito, com uma flora proveniente do meio natural e plantando árvores que poderiam ser parte
integrante de um bosque selvagem. Neste sentido, alguns dos exemplos aqui apresentados procuram o mimetismo com o ambiente, numa tentativa de reproduzir a paisagem natural que os rodeia.

As estratégias utilizadas pelos desenhadores e arquitectos recolhidas neste livro chamam a atenção para os recursos disponíveis para que o jardim se integre no nosso habitat e, deste modo, compense o quotidiano dominado pelo asfalto e carente de espaços verdes públicos. Conservar os espaços naturais periurbanos ou potenciar as zonas verdes urbanas deveria ser uma prioridade nos futuros planos urbanísticos das nossas cidades e um aspecto essencial para a valorização da paisagem urbana e da qualidade de vida dos cidadãos.

Konst, jordbruk och ekologi är de tre grundidéerna som de nya trenderna inom nutidens utomhusdesign kretsar kring. I själva verket rör det sig inte om en ny brytande strömning. Det handlar om det traditionella konceptet att skapa och bevara trädgårdsutrymmen, och att göra detta så att det passar ihop med andra nutida sätt att uppfatta trädgårdar. De
gröna utrymmena har gått från att endast vara ett estetiskt bidrag till landskapet, till att bli till ett huvudinslag inom hållbar utveckling och miljö.

Boken presenterar olika uterum som delats upp utifrån typ: terrasser, balkonger, innergårdar och takträdgårdar; projekt som är uppbyggda kring de arbetssätt som utgör den moderna trädgårdens mest representativa trender. Det nutida i de olika förslagen har sin grund i här nya sättet att göra utomhusdesign, som kallas "agritektur", en harmonisk symbios mellan konstruktion, levande miljö och mänsklig aktivitet. Det är det senare som blir en avgörande faktor vid skapandet av ett uterum som anpassas efter var och ens behov. Det frenetiska stadslivet har gjort de gröna rummen till platser för nedvarvning, framförallt de som är en del av bostaden. De har fler förtjänster än en isolerad trädgård. Att de återfinns i mellanutrymmen gör dem till en mikrokosmos som hjälper till att öka livskvaliteten för storstadens invånare. Avsaknaden av utrymme, bristen på bördig jord, tidsbrist och brist på ljus brukar känneteckna de här svårplanerade trädgårdarna. Trots detta har nutida byggnadsteknik, material och utrustning utan tvekan förvandlat dem till ytterligare ett beboeligt rum, vid sidan om de andra rummen i bostaden. Dessutom har respekten för miljön och utnyttjandet av tillgängliga naturresurser lite i taget blivit prioritet för att garantera hållbarhet i trädgårdsutrymmet. Att återanvända vattnet är grundläggande för att uppnå ekologisk balans. Ett exempel på detta visar sig hos några av projekten som presenteras längre fram, med byggandet av dammar eller vattensystem för att ta vara på regnvattnet när man bevattnar trädgården.

Strävan efter att återvända till naturen leder till skapandet av uterum som ligger mycket nära ett fritt och rikt växtliv. Man försöker skapa en känsla av vilda platser, med en flora som härrör direkt från naturen och genom att använda sig av träd som skulle kunna finnas i en regnskog. På det här sättet strävar några av de här presenterade exemplen efter att skydda sig i omgivningens förklädnad genom att efterlikna det omgivande ursprungslandskapet.

Strategierna som använts av designerna och arkitekterna i den här boken framhäver de resurser som kan integrera en trädgård i vår miljö och, på detta sätt, kompensera den av asfalt dominerade vardagligheten, som lider brist på gröna offentliga platser. Att bevara naturliga områden runt staden och ge kraft åt gröna ytor i staden borde prioriteras vid framtida stadsplanering, samt borde vara en grundläggande aspekt när man vill förbättra stadsmiljön och livskvaliteten för invånarna.

TERRACES

TERRASSES · TERRASSEN · TERRASSEN · TERRAZAS · TERRAZZE · TERRAÇOS · TERRASSER

It is not hard to turn a terrace into a small garden. A multitude of solutions are available today to transform a terrace into an alternative space in which to enjoy almost rural-like moments of peace and calm. Turning a terrace into an al fresco dining room in spring and summer, a corner for get-togethers, or a small vegetable garden are some ways to make a pleasant environment next to the home. One good idea is to install a fountain or pond with a circuit that recycles water. The climate and layout of the terrain will indicate the most suitable types of plants.

Ce n'est pas difficile de transformer une terrasse en verger. Il existe aujourd'hui de nombreuses solutions pour convertir les terrasses en un espace alternatif où profiter de moments sereins et tranquilles, presque champêtres. Faire de la terrasse une salle à manger pour le printemps et l'été, un coin pour les réunions ou un petit potager permet d'obtenir un environnement agréable près de la maison. L'installation d'une fontaine ou d'un étang avec un circuit qui recycle l'eau est une idée saine. Le climat et la disposition du terrain détermineront le type de plantes le mieux adapté.

Es ist gar nicht so schwer, eine Terrasse in einen blühenden Garten zu verwandeln. Heute stehen einem vielfältige Lösungen zur Verfügung, wenn man seine Terrasse in einen Raum zur Entspannung in fast ländlicher Ruhe umgestalten möchte. Zweifellos wird der Wohnwert jedes Heims durch einen Essplatz unter freiem Himmel, eine Sitzgruppe für ungezwungene Gespräche oder einen kleinen Nutzgarten erheblich gesteigert. Sehr zu empfehlen ist auch die Anlage eines kleinen Springbrunnens oder eines Teichs zur Wasseraufbereitung. Die Auswahl der Bepflanzung hängt von Klima und Lage der Terrasse ab.

Het is niet moeilijk om een terras te veranderen in een kleine lusthof. Tegenwoordig zijn er allerlei mogelijkheden om van terrassen ruimten te maken waar van een bijna landelijke rust kan worden genoten. Een terras kan worden omgetoverd tot een eethoek voor in de lente en zomer, tot een vergaderplek of een kleine moestuin. Het zijn allemaal benaderingen om van een buitenruimte een prettig verlengstuk van het huis te maken. Fonteinen of vijvers met een watercirculatiesysteem zijn nuttig. Klimaat en omgeving zijn bepalend bij de keuze van de planten.

No es difícil convertir una terraza en un pequeño vergel. Hoy en día hay múltiples soluciones para transformar las terrazas en un espacio alternativo en el que disfrutar de momentos de paz y tranquilidad casi campestres. Convertir la terraza en un comedor de primavera y verano, en un rincón para reuniones o en un pequeño huerto es una forma de conseguir un entorno agradable junto a la vivienda. Una idea saludable es instalar una fuente o un estanque con un circuito que recicle el agua. El clima y la disposición del terreno indicarán la tipología de plantas más adecuada.

Non è difficile trasformare una terrazza in un piccolo paradiso. Esistono oggi molte soluzioni per trasformare questi spazi in luoghi alternativi in cui godersi momenti di pace e tranquillità quasi bucoliche. Convertire la terrazza in una zona pranzo per la primavera e l'estate, in un angolo per stare con gli amici o in un piccolo orto è un modo di avere un ambiente gradevole accanto all'abitazione. Un'ottima idea consiste nell'installare una fontanella o un bacino con un circuito che ricicla l'acqua. Il clima e la disposizione del terreno indicheranno la tipologia di piante più adatta.

Não é difícil converter um terraço num pequeno pomar. Hoje em dia há múltiplas soluções para transformar os terraços num espaço alternativo para nele desfrutar momentos de paz e tranquilidade quase campestres. Transformar o terraço numa sala de jantar para a Primavera e o Verão, num recanto para reuniões ou num pequeno jardim permite criar um ambiente agradável junto à residência. Uma boa medida é instalar uma fonte ou um tanque com um circuito de renovação da água. O clima e a disposição do terreno indicarão o tipo de plantas mais adequado.

Det är inte svårt att förvandla en terrass till en liten trädgård. Nuförtiden finns det ett flertal lösningar för den som vill omvandla terrasser till ett alternativt utrymme för fridfulla och lugna stunder av nästan lantlig karaktär. Att göra om terrassen till en matsal på sommaren och våren, till en mötespunkt eller till en liten odling, är ett sätt att uppnå en trivsam miljö i anslutning till bostaden. En välgörande idé är att placera en källa eller damm med fontän där vattnet får cirkulera. Klimatet och områdets utseende får bestämma vilken typ av växter som passar.

HOUSE IN **LAS ARENAS**

ARTADI ARQUITECTOS
www.javierartadi.com
© Alexander Kornhuber

A transport container was the starting point for designing this residence 60 miles south of Lima. By raising the main box-like section, the building appears to float above the land. A terrace with a long sofa and table with sea views is the most important space in the home, giving onto the deserted coastline that surrounds it in search of tranquility.

Un container de transport a été le point de départ de la conception de cette résidence située à 100 km au sud de Lima. Du fait de l'élévation de la section principale, similaire à une boîte, le bâtiment semble flotter sur le sol. Une terrasse, avec un grand canapé et une table avec vue sur la mer, est la pièce la plus importante de la demeure qui s'ouvre sur le littoral désertique qui l'entoure, en quête de tranquillité.

Dieses Haus liegt etwa 100 km südlich von Lima und erinnert an einen großen Container. Der Baukörper scheint über dem Boden zu schweben. Die Öffnung hin zur Ruhe der umgebenden Landschaft ist das wichtigste Merkmal dieses Hauses: Eine Terrasse mit einem lang gestreckten Sofa und einem Tisch lässt den Ausblick auf den wüstenartigen Küstenstreifen zum unvergesslichen Erlebnis werden.

Een container vormde het uitgangspunt voor het ontwerp van deze woning die 100 km ten zuiden van Lima ligt. Door het belangrijkste deel – dat op een kist lijkt – te verhogen, lijkt het bouwwerk boven de grond te zweven. Met een grote bank en een tafel is een terras met uitzicht op zee de belangrijkste ruimte van de woning, die ter wille van de rust op de verlaten kuststrook is georiënteerd.

Un contenedor de transporte fue el punto de partida para diseñar esta residencia situada 100 km al sur de Lima. Al elevar la sección principal, similar a una caja, la edificación parece flotar sobre el suelo. La terraza, con un largo sofá y una mesa desde los que disfrutar de magníficas vistas, es la estancia más importante de la vivienda, y se abre al litoral desértico en busca de tranquilidad.

L'ispirazione per progettare questa residenza, situata a 100 km a sud di Lima, è venuta dalla forma di un container. Grazie al sollevamento della sezione principale, simile a una scatola, l'edificio sembra sospeso. Una terrazza con un lungo sofà, un tavolo e una magnifica vista sul mare è l'area più importante di una casa concepita alla ricerca della tranquillità, sul litorale desertico che la circonda.

Um contentor de transporte foi o ponto de partida para o projecto desta residência a 100 km ao sul de Lima. O modo como a espécie de caixa, se ergue sobre o solo cria a impressão de flutuar. Decorado com um longo sofá e uma mesa, o terraço com vista para o mar é o espaço mais importante da residência, que se abre sobre o litoral desértico que a rodeia, em busca de tranquilidade.

En container var utgångspunkten för utformandet av denna bostad som ligger 100 km söder om Lima. Genom att placera huvuddelen, en lådliknande konstruktion, högre upp, ser byggnaden ut att sväva ovanför marken. En terrass med en lång soffa och ett bord med havsutsikt utgör det viktigaste rummet i bostaden, som öppnar sig mot den omgivande öde havskusten på jakt efter lugn.

Underground plan

Terrace plan

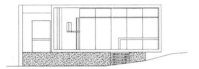

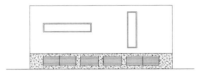

Façade sections

HOUSE IN **BRICKELL-POLLOCK**

HOPKINSON TEAM ARCHITECTURE
www.teamarchitecture.co.nz
© Simon Devitt

This vacation home sits on the peak of a hill on the western side of New Zealand's North Island. The house's orientation was determined by the views over the Tasman Sea and the forest of white tea (kanuka) trees. The main spaces are connected by porches that afford a protected exterior space. The terrace runs east-west to make the most of the sun.

Cette résidence de vacances est située au sommet d'une colline à l'ouest de l'Ile du Nord en Nouvelle-Zélande. L'orientation de la maison a été déterminée par la vue sur la mer de Tasmanie et la forêt d'arbres à thé blanc *(kanuka)*. Les principaux espaces sont reliés par des porches offrant un espace extérieur protégé. Afin de profiter au maximum du soleil, la terrasse s'étend d'est en ouest.

Dieses Feriendomizil liegt auf dem Gipfel eines Hügels im Westen der Nordinsel Neuseelands. Die Ausrichtung des Hauses wurde von der Aussicht auf die Tasmansee und einen Wald aus weißen Teebäumen (Kanuka) bestimmt. Die Haupträume sind durch überdachte Gänge witterungsunabhängig miteinander verbunden. Um das Sonnenlicht optimal zu nutzen, liegt die Terrasse in Ost-West-Richtung.

Deze vakantiewoning staat boven op een heuvel ten westen van het Noordereiland van NieuwZeeland. De ligging wordt bepaald door het uitzicht op de Tasmanzee en het bos van witte theebomen (kanuka). De hoofdvertrekken zijn met elkaar verbonden via galerijen die beschutte buitenruimte bieden. Om optimaal van de zon te profiteren is het terras zowel in oostelijke als in westelijke richting aangelegd.

Esta residencia de vacaciones está situada en la cima de una colina, en la parte occidental de la Isla Norte, en Nueva Zelanda. Las vistas al mar de Tasmania y el bosque de árboles de té blanco *(kanuka)* determinaron la orientación de la casa. Los principales espacios están conectados por porches que ofrecen un espacio exterior protegido. Para aprovechar al máximo el sol, la terraza se extiende hacia el este y el oeste.

Questa casa di vacanze sta sulla cima di una collina nella parte occidentale dell'Isola del Nord, in Nuova Zelanda. L'orientazione è stata concepita in base alle viste sul mare di Tasmania e sul bosco di alberi di tè bianco *kanuka*. Gli spazi principali sono uniti da portici, che creano uno spazio esterno riparato. Per sfruttare al massimo la luce del sole, la terrazza ha un'orientazione est-ovest.

Esta residência de férias está situada no cimo de uma colina a oeste da Ilha Norte da Nova Zelândia. A orientação da casa foi determinada pela vista sobre o mar da Tasmânia e sobre o bosque de árvores de chá branco *(kanuka)*. As principais áreas comunicam através de alpendres que oferecem um espaço protegido embora exterior. Para aproveitar o máximo de Sol, o terraço estende-se de nascente para poente.

Den här semesterbostaden ligger på toppen av en kulle på västra sidan av Norrön på Nya Zeeland. Husets läge avgjordes av utsikten över Tasmansjön och skogen av kanuka-träd, av vilka man producerar vitt te. De viktigaste utrymmena kopplas samman genom verandor som erbjuder ett uterum med tak. För att utnyttja solljuset på bästa sätt breder terrassen ut sig mot både öst och väst.

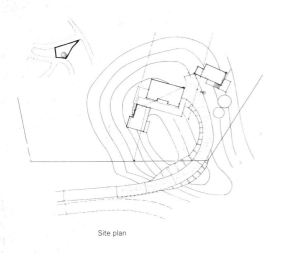

Site plan

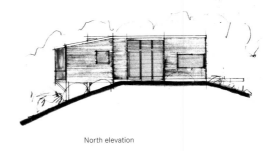

North elevation

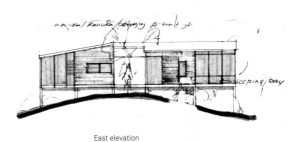

East elevation

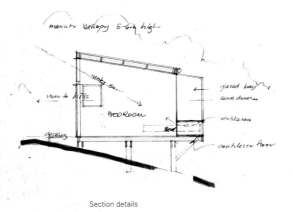

Section details

North elevation studio

This building is a perfect example of an environmentally friendly construction and incorporates sustainable-design strategies. Protection from direct sunlight and optimal views were the parameters that influenced the distribution of the spaces: the southwest façade is exposed to the afternoon light, while the northeast face is fully glassed-in to make the most of the spectacular views.

Ce bâtiment est un parfait exemple de construction respectueuse de l'environnement qui intègre des stratégies de design durables. La protection de la lumière solaire directe et un meilleur panorama ont été les paramètres qui ont influé sur la répartition des espaces : la façade qui donne au sud-ouest est exposée au soleil l'après-midi, tandis que la face nord est entièrement vitrée afin de profiter de la vue fantastique.

Dieses Gebäude ist ein hervorragendes Beispiel für umweltverträgliches Bauen. Der Entwurf steht im Zeichen der Nachhaltigkeit: Der Schutz vor der Sonneneinstrahlung und der Erhalt der besten Sichtachsen bestimmten die Anlage der Innenräume. Die Südwestfassade liegt am Nachmittag in der Sonne, während die Nordostseite vollständig verglast wurde, um die atemberaubende Aussicht genießen zu können.

Dit gebouw is een uitstekend voorbeeld van milieuvriendelijk bouwen waarbij duurzame ontwerpmethoden zijn gebruikt. De bescherming tegen rechtstreeks zonlicht en een mooi uitzicht bepaalden mede de indeling van de ruimten: de gevel op het zuidwesten krijgt 's middags zon, terwijl de noordoostkant helemaal van glas is zodat men van het spectaculaire uitzicht kan genieten.

Este edificio es un perfecto ejemplo de edificación respetuosa con el medio ambiente e incorpora estrategias de diseño sostenibles. La distribución de los espacios se realizó con los objetivos de proteger de la luz solar directa y ofrecer las mejores vistas: la fachada que da al suroeste se encuentra expuesta a la luz de la tarde, mientras que la cara noreste está totalmente acristalada para disfrutar del magnífico paisaje.

Questo immobile è un perfetto esempio di edilizia rispettosa dell'ambiente e incorpora strategie di design sostenibile. La distribuzione degli spazi è stata realizzata secondo criteri quali la protezione dalla luce solare diretta e le viste: la facciata che dà a sudovest è esposta alla luce del pomeriggio, mentre il lato nordest è tutto a vetri così da poter ammirare il paesaggio.

Este edifício é um exemplo de construção amiga do ambiente e da incorporação de estratégias arquitectónicas sustentáveis. A protecção contra a incidência directa da luz solar e a melhor vista panorâmica foram determinantes para a distribuição dos espaços: a fachada virada a sudoeste recebe a luz durante a tarde, enquanto a virada para nordeste é totalmente envidraçada para o usufruto das vistas espectaculares.

Den här byggnaden är ett perfekt exempel på en konstruktion som respekterar miljön och införlivar strategier för hållbar design. Bevarandet av det direkta solljuset och den finaste utsikten var utgångspunkter som påverkade planlösningar; fasaden som vetter mot sydöst får eftermiddagsljus, medan den nordöstliga sidan är helt inglasad för att det ska gå att njuta av den fantastiska utsikten.

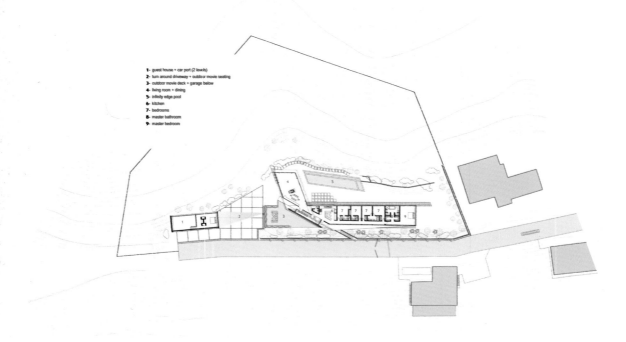

1- guest house + car port (2 levels)
2- turn around driveway + outdoor movie seating
3- outdoor movie deck + garage below
4- living room + dining
5- infinity edge pool
6- kitchen
7- bedrooms
8- master bathroom
9- master bedroom

Site plan

Natural ventilation diagrams

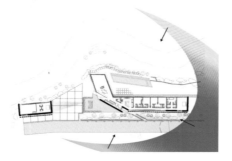

Orientation: solar angles, viewing angles and daylighting diagram

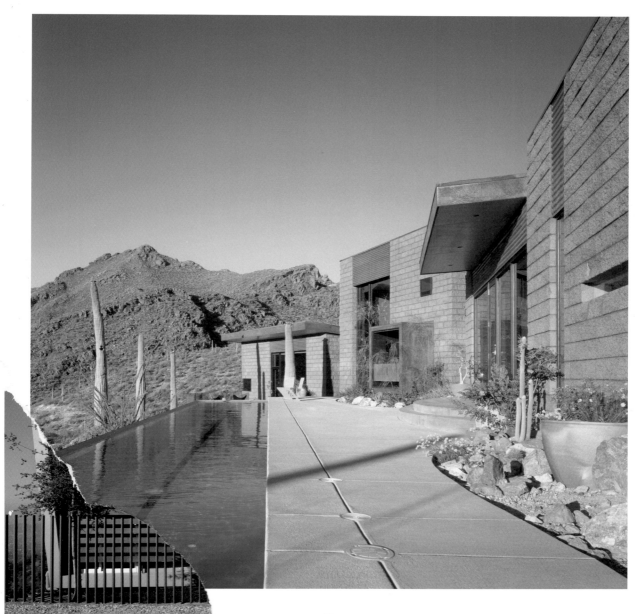

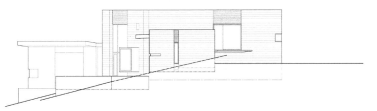

Northeast elevation

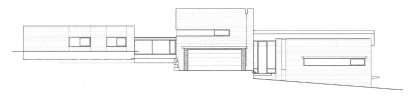

Northwest elevation

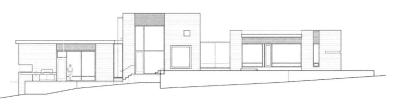

Southeast elevation

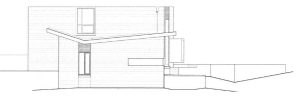

Southwest elevation

RUSSELL CLETTA
www.russcletta.com
© Undine Prohl

This garden in LA's San Fernando Valley was designed as an outdoor entertainment area for friends and clients. The garden, with its hearty-leafed plants and perennials in dark green, silver and chartreuse, is a quiet spot in which to take refuge from the city. A lime-colored trellis dissimulates the outdoor lights and heaters and also functions as an overhead structure for the grapevine that covers the terrace-cum-dining area.

Ce jardin situé à San Fernando Valley, à Los Angeles, a été planifié comme un espace de divertissement extérieur pour amis et clients. Le jardin, avec des plantes à feuilles vivaces et persistantes dans les tons vert sombre, argenté et chartreuse, est un lieu tranquille où se réfugier pour échapper à la ville. Un grillage de couleur vert lime dissimule l'éclairage et les chauffages extérieurs et sert également de structure aérienne pour la vigne couvrant la terrasse-salle à manger.

Dieser Garten liegt im San Fernando Valley nahe Los Angeles und dient Freunden und Kunden der Eigentümer als ein Ort der Entspannung, an dem man sich fern der Stadt erholen kann, umgeben von den immergrünen Pflanzen mit ihren dunkel, silbrig oder leuchtend grünen Blättern. Lampen und Außenheizung verschwinden hinter dem limettengrün gestrichenen Gitternetz, das als Rankhilfe für die Pergola über dem Essplatz dient.

Deze tuin in San Fernando Valley, Los Angeles, moest dienen als ontspanningsruimte voor vrienden en klanten. Met zijn planten met groenblijvend zilverkleurig en geelgroen blad is de tuin een oase van rust waarin men de stad kan ontvluchten. Het limoenkleurige latwerk dempt het licht en de warmte, en fungeert bovendien als een steun voor de wingerd boven de eethoek op het terras.

Este jardín situado en San Fernando Valley, en Los Ángeles, se proyectó como un espacio de diversión exterior para amigos y clientes. El jardín, con sus plantas de hojas vivaces y perennes de colores verde oscuro, plateado y pistacho, es un lugar tranquilo donde poder refugiarse de la ciudad. Un enrejado de color lima disimula las luces y los calefactores exteriores, además de funcionar como estructura aérea para la parra que cubre la terraza-comedor.

Questo giardino sito nella San Fernando Valley, a Los Angeles, con le sue piante dalle foglie perenni e i vivaci toni verde scuro, argentato e lime, è stato concepito come un luogo di svago per amici e clienti che vogliono fuggire dalla città. Un reticolato di color lima occulta parzialmente le luci e le stufe esterne, oltre a fungere da supporto per la vite che copre la terrazza-zona pranzo.

Este jardim de San Fernando Valley, em Los Angeles, foi projectado como um espaço exterior de ócio para amigos e clientes. Com plantas vivazes e perenes de folhagem em tons de verde-escuro, prateado e verde-esmeralda, é um lugar tranquilo para fugir ao bulício da cidade. Um entrelaçado de cor verde-limão dissimula os focos de luz e os aquecedores exteriores, e sustenta a parreira que cobre a parte do terraço reservada a refeições.

Den här trädgården i San Fernando Valley, i Los Ángeles, var tänkt som ett uppehållsrum utomhus för vänner och kunder. Trädgården, med växter med långlivade blad och perenner i mörkgrönt, silverfärger och gulgrönt är en lugn plats där man kan fly undan staden. Ett limegrönt spjälverk döljer lamporna och infravärmen utomhus, utöver att fungera som stöd för vinrankorna på matsalsterrassen.

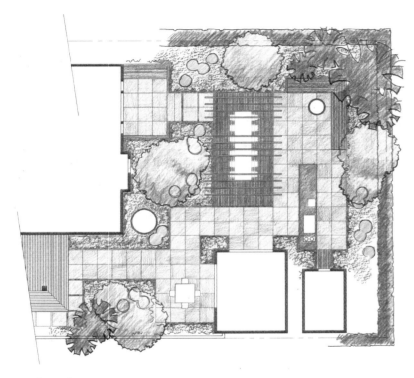

Terrace plan

HARIRI & HARIRI ARCHITECTURE
www.haririandhariri.com
© Paul Warchol

Floating above a 47x20-ft swimming pool like a boat in the sea, this 1,200-sq-ft structure contains a spa and an indoor/outdoor shower. It also has a covered balcony which serves as an interior/exterior dining room, with a wall that features an opening that frames the landscape. The area around the pool, covered in travertine tiles and with stone steps, becomes a lower-level patio.

Flottant sur une piscine de 14,5 x 6 m comme un bateau sur l'eau, cette structure de 111 m² contient un spa et une douche d'intérieur/extérieur. Elle dispose en outre d'une galerie couverte, qui sert de couloir intérieur/extérieur, et sur son mur se détache une ouverture encadrant le paysage. La zone qui entoure la piscine, revêtue de travertin et dotée de marches en pierre, se transforme en cour à un niveau inférieur.

Über einem 14,5 x 6 m großen Schwimmbecken schwebt eine 111 m² große Konstruktion, die eine Außendusche und einen Badekomplex umfasst. Ein überdachter Raum dient als Essplatz zu jeder Jahreszeit; ein Fenster in der Wand rahmt die dahinter liegende Landschaft wie ein Bild ein. Der mit Travertin ausgelegte Bereich um das Schwimmbecken mit seiner steinernen Treppe wird zu einem tiefer gelegenen Patio.

In dit bouwwerk van 111 m² dat als een schip op zee boven een zwembad van 14,5 x 6 meter zweeft, zijn een spa en een douche ondergebracht. Daarnaast is er een overdekte galerij die dienstdoet als eethoek binnen en buiten. Opvallend is de muuropening waardoor het landschap te zien is. De ruimte rond het met travertijn beklede zwembad met stenen treden fungeert een verdieping lager als patio.

Flotando sobre una piscina de 14,5 x 6 m como un barco en el mar, esta estructura de 111 m² contiene un *spa* y una ducha de interior y exterior. Además dispone de una galería techada que sirve como comedor, en cuya pared destaca una abertura que enmarca el paisaje. El área que rodea la piscina, revestida de travertino y con escalones de piedra, se convierte en patio a un nivel inferior.

Questa struttura di 111 m², che galleggia su una piscina di 14,5 x 6 m, contiene uno *spa* e una doccia interna/esterna. Possiede, inoltre, una loggia coperta che funge da zona pranzo, lungo la parete della quale spicca un'apertura che fa da cornice al paesaggio. L'area circostante, rivestita di travertino e con gradini di pietra, diventa un cortile a un livello sottostante.

Flutuando sobre uma piscina de 14,5 x 6 m, como um barco em pleno mar, esta estrutura de 111 m² contém um *spa* e um chuveiro de interior e de exterior. Dispõe ainda de uma galeria coberta para refeições, e em cuja parede se destaca uma abertura a emoldurar a paisagem envolvente. A rodear a piscina, uma área revestida de travertino e com degraus de pedra, converte-se num pátio a um nível inferior.

Den här 111 m² stora konstruktionen, som flyter på en 14,5 x 6 m stor pool likt en båt på havet, har ett spa och en dusch inomhus/utomhus. Dessutom har den ett utrymme med tak som fungerar som matsal både inomhus och utomhus. På en av väggarna framträder en öppning som ramar in landskapet. Området runt poolen, som beklätts med travertin och som fått trappsteg av sten, blir till en liten patio.

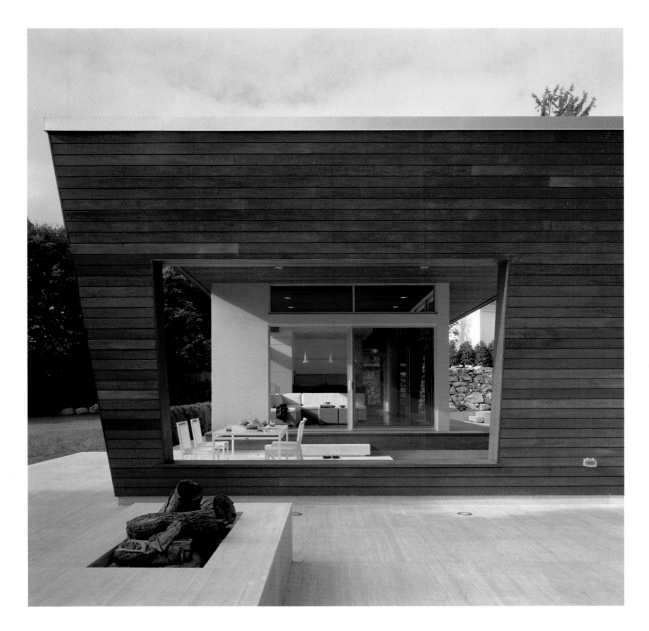

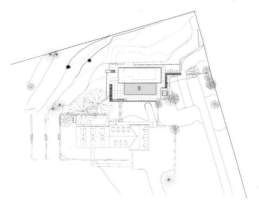

Site plan

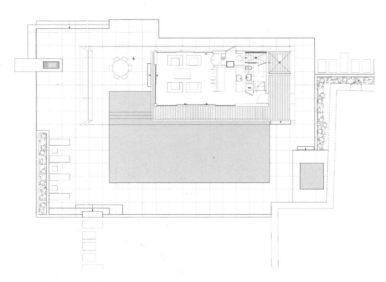

Plan

HOUSE **IN THE FOREST**

STUDIO ARTHUR CASAS
www.arthurcasas.com
© Richard Powers

The spaces in this house are in complete synergy with the exterior. Two large symmetrical cubes surround an open central area with 36-ft-high glass windows at both ends that capture the exterior landscape. To seek harmony with the magnificent surroundings, the house is covered in Cumaru wood panels. The absence of dividing walls helps the house merge into the surrounding landscape and adds a spectacular element to the minimalist interiors.

Les espaces de cette maison sont en totale synergie avec l'extérieur. Deux grands cubes symétriques enveloppent une zone ouverte centrale, avec des baies vitrées de 11 mètres de hauteur, ce qui permet de voir le paysage extérieur. Dans une optique d'harmonie avec l'environnement magnifique, la maison est revêtue de panneaux en bois de coumarou. L'absence de divisions favorise la fusion entre la maison et les alentours et ajoute un élément spectaculaire aux intérieurs minimalistes.

Dieses Haus steht völlig im Einklang mit der Umgebung. Zwei große symmetrische Kuben umschließen einen offenen zentralen Bereich mit elf Meter hohen Fenstern auf beiden Seiten, durch die man hinaus sieht. Das Haus ist mit Kumaruholz verkleidet, um es der Natur anzupassen. Der Verzicht auf Trennwände in den minimalistisch gestalteten Innenräumen betont die Verschmelzung von Drinnen und Draußen.

Er is synergie tussen binnen en buiten. Twee grote symmetrische blokken omvatten de centrale open ruimte met opzij ramen van 11 meter hoog, waardoor het landschap binnenkomt. Om in harmonie met de fraaie omgeving te zijn is het huis bekleed met panelen van cumaruhout. Doordat er geen afscheidingen zijn, lopen huis en omgeving zo in elkaar over en krijgt het interieur er een minimalistisch element bij.

Los espacios de esta casa están en total sinergia con el exterior. Dos grandes cubos simétricos envuelven un área abierta central con ventanas de cristal de 11 metros de altura en ambos extremos, captando así el paisaje exterior. Para buscar la armonía con el magnífico entorno, la casa está revestida de paneles de madera de cumarú. La ausencia de divisiones favorece la fusión entre la casa y los alrededores, y añade un elemento espectacular a los interiores minimalistas.

Questa casa è in sinergia con l'esterno. Due grandi cubi simmetrici avvolgono un'area centrale con finestre di vetro alte 11 metri, a entrambe le estremità. Per stabilire un rapporto armonico con l'ambiente circostante, la casa è rivestita di pannelli di legno cumarù. L'assenza di divisioni favorisce la fusione con i dintorni e dà un elemento spettacolare agli interni in stile minimalista.

Os espaços desta casa estão em total sinergia com o exterior. Dois grandes cubos simétricos determinam uma área central com janelas envidraçadas de 11 metros de altura em ambos os extremos, para assim captar a paisagem exterior. Para se integrar em harmonia com o magnífico ambiente que a rodeia, a casa está revestida de painéis de madeira. A ausência de divisões favorece a união entre a casa minimalista e o meio envolvente.

Rummen samverkar här helt och hållet med utemiljön. Två stora symmetriska kuber omsluter en öppen yta med 11 meter höga fönster, som fångar det yttre landskapet. För att uppnå harmoni med den fantastiska miljön har huset beklätts med paneler av cumaro- trä. Frånvaron av uppdelningar framhäver fusionen mellan huset och omgivningen och tillför ett spektakulärt inslag i den minimalistiska interiören.

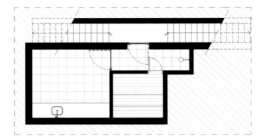

Basement plan

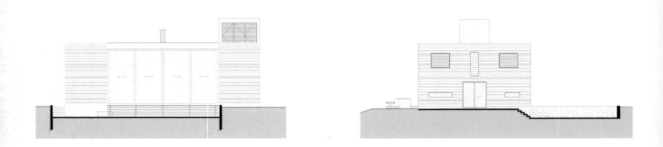

Sections

AMIR SCHLEZINGER/MYLANDSCAPES
www.mylandscapes.co.uk
© Tim Soar

The white walls and wooden floor recall the ocean liners of days gone by. A carpet of artificial grass expresses the owner's desire to enjoy the outdoor space year-round. The plants must be leafy and keep their beauty throughout the year: box, yucca, lavender, and agave turn green anew over the course of the seasons and can handle the extreme conditions of a terrace like this.

Les murs blancs et le sol en bois nous rappellent les transatlantiques d'antan. Un tapis en gazon artificiel traduit le désir du propriétaire de profiter de l'espace extérieur à n'importe quelle saison. Les plantes doivent être luxuriantes et rester belles toute l'année : le buis, le yucca, la lavande et l'agave reverdissent au cours des saisons et peuvent supporter les conditions extrêmes d'une terrasse comme celle-ci.

Weiße Wände und Holzdeck erinnern an die früheren Ozeanriesen der Transatlantikroute. Der Teppich aus Kunstrasen zeigt, dass der Eigentümer diesen Außenbereich ganzjährig nutzt. Die Bepflanzung ist gewollt üppig und das ganze Jahr über attraktiv: Buchsbaum, Yucca, Lavendel und Agave sind immergrün und widerstehen den extremen Witterungsbedingungen, die auf einer solchen Terrasse herrschen.

De witte muren en houten vloer doen denken aan de vroegere oceaanstomers. In het tapijt van kunstgras wordt de wens van de eigenaar weerspiegeld om elk seizoen van de buitenruimte te kunnen genieten. De weelderige vegetatie is het hele jaar mooi: buxus, yuca, lavendel en agave zijn het hele jaar groen en zijn goed bestand tegen de extreme omstandigheden die op dit terras heersen.

Las paredes blancas y el suelo de madera nos recuerdan a los transatlánticos de antaño. Una alfombra de césped artificial expresa el deseo del propietario de disfrutar del espacio exterior en cualquier estación. Las plantas deben ser frondosas y mantenerse atractivas todo el año: el boj, la yuca, la lavanda y la pita reverdecen a lo largo de las estaciones y pueden soportar las extremas condiciones de una terraza como esta.

Le pareti bianche e il pavimento di legno ricordano i transatlantici d'epoca. Un tappeto d'erba artificiale esprime il desiderio del proprietario di godere dello spazio esterno in qualsiasi stagione. Le piante devono essere frondose e restare belle tutto l'anno: il bosso, la yucca, la lavanda e l'agave rinverdiscono nel corso delle stagioni e sopportano le estreme condizioni di una terrazza come questa.

As paredes brancas e o chão de madeira lembram os transatlânticos do passado. Um tapete de relva artificial revela o desejo do proprietário de desfrutar do exterior em qualquer época do ano. Na concretização desse desejo, as plantas são frondosas e mantêm um aspecto atraente durante o ano inteiro: o buxo, a iuca, a alfazema e a piteira resistem e suportam bem as condições climáticas extremas de um terraço como este.

De vita väggarna och trägolvet påminner oss om atlantångarna från förr. En matta av konstgräs uttrycker ägarens önskan om att njuta av uterummet året runt. Växterna bör vara lummiga och hålla sig vackra hela året: buxbom, palmlilja, lavendel och agaver får nytt liv i takt med att årstiderna byter av varandra och klarar den här typen av terrassers extrema förhållanden.

PATRICK GENARD
www.patrickgenard.com
© Pere Planells

This garden pertains to a house built between dividing walls. The elongated swimming pool is set in one corner of the elegant garden. Running longitudinally along the bottom half of the wall is a rectangular white module containing different plants and incorporating a rectangular spout from which water streams. The rectangular shapes are softened by the spongy carpet of grass and the tropical timber roof that extends through to the water.

Ce jardin appartient à une maison mitoyenne. La piscine allongée se situe dans un coin du jardin sobre. Dans la partie inférieure du mur, longitudinalement, se situe un module blanc rectangulaire contenant différentes plantes et intégrant un tuyau rectangulaire d'où coule de l'eau. Les formes rectangulaires sont adoucies par le tapis de gazon moelleux et la toiture en bois tropical qui se prolonge jusqu'à l'eau.

Dieser Garten gehört zu einem Reihenhaus. Das längliche Schwimmbecken liegt in einer Ecke des schlichten Gartens. Unten an der Längswand befindet sich ein weißer, länglicher Kasten mit verschiedenen Pflanzen und einem Vierkantrohr, aus dem Wasser strömt. Die rechteckigen Formen stehen in kontrastreicher Spannung zum weichen Rasenteppich und dem Deck aus Tropenholz, das bis zum Wasser führt.

Deze tuin hoort bij een huis dat tussen gemeenschappelijke muren staat. Het langwerpige zwembad ligt in een hoek van de sobere tuin. In de lengterichting van het lage deel van de muur bevindt zich een rechthoekig wit element met planten en een rechthoekige buis waar water uit opwelt. De rechthoekige vormen worden verzacht door het gazon en de overkapping van tropisch hout die tot het water reikt.

Este jardín pertenece a una casa construida entre medianeras. La piscina alargada se sitúa en una esquina del sobrio jardín. En la parte inferior de la pared, longitudinalmente, hay un módulo blanco rectangular que contiene diferentes plantas y que incorpora un caño rectangular del que mana agua. Las formas rectangulares se suavizan con la mullida alfombra de césped y con la cubierta de madera tropical que llega hasta el agua.

Questo giardino appartiene a una casa costruita tra due edifici. La piscina occupa un angolo del giardino. Nella parte inferiore della parete, corre longitudinalmente un modulo bianco rettangolare che contiene diverse piante e incorpora un condotto da cui sgorga acqua. Le forme rettangolari sono ammorbidite dal soffice tappeto erboso e dal tetto di legno tropicale che arriva fino all'acqua.

Este jardim pertence a uma casa construída entre outras duas. A piscina alongada situa-se num canto do sóbrio jardim. Ao longo de toda a parte inferior da parede, um módulo branco rectangular contendo diferentes plantas incorpora um cano rectangular donde flui água. A rigidez das formas rectangulares suaviza-se com o fofo tapete de relva e com a cobertura de madeira tropical que chega até à água.

Den här trädgården tillhör ett hus som byggts mellan murar. Den långsmala poolen ligger i ett hörn av den diskreta trädgården. Längs med väggens lägre del finns en vit, rektangulär modul med olika växter och som införlivar ett fyrkantigt rör med flödande vatten. De rektangulära formerna mildras med hjälp av den fluffiga mattan av gräs och taket av tropiskt trä som når ända till vattnet.

BAMBÚ GARDEN

A glass door enables access to the terrace, increasing the feeling of inhabitable space inside. With the same goal in mind, the size of the windows enables light to enter any time of day. The terrace is limited by wooden panels on one side, while on the other an alignment of dry reeds next to decorative bamboo stalks separates it from the neighbors.

Une porte vitrée permet d'accéder à la terrasse, ce qui accentue la sensation de surface habitable à l'intérieur. Dans le même objectif, la taille des fenêtres permet à la lumière de pénétrer à toute heure de la journée. D'un côté, la terrasse est limitée par des panneaux en bois et, de l'autre, un alignement décoratif de roseaux séchés et de tiges de bambou la séparent des voisins.

Durch eine Glastür gelangt man auf die Terrasse, die so als eine Erweiterung des Wohnraums wahrgenommen wird. Die großen Fenster verfolgen den gleichen Zweck: sie lassen das Tageslicht herein und erlauben die Sicht hinaus. Die Terrasse wird auf der einen Seite von Holzpanelen begrenzt, auf der anderen schützt eine Wand aus Bambus und Schilfrohr vor den neugierigen Blicken der Nachbarn.

Een glazen deur geeft toegang tot het terras, waardoor het gevoel van ruimtelijkheid in huis groter wordt. De afmetingen van de ramen, die op elk uur van de dag voor daglicht zorgen, versterken dit gevoel nog eens. Aan één kant wordt het terras begrensd door houten panelen. Aan de andere kant is er een afscheiding van decoratieve bamboe- en rietstengels.

Una puerta de cristal conduce a la terraza, aumentando así la sensación de superficie habitable en el interior. Para reforzar esta idea, la dimensión de las ventanas permite la entrada de luz a cualquier hora del día. Por un lado, la terraza está limitada por paneles de madera; por el otro, una alineación de cañas secas junto a cañas de bambú decorativas la separa de los vecinos.

Alla terrazza si accede mediante una porta di vetro, che dall'interno aumenta la sensazione di superficie abitabile. Perseguendo il medesimo fine, la dimensione delle finestre permette l'entrata di luce a qualsiasi ora del giorno. La terrazza è delimitata, da una parte, mediante pannelli di legno e, dall'altra, con una fila di canne secche, accanto a decorative canne di bambù.

A porta em vidro que dá acesso ao terraço gera a sensação do aumento de habitabilidade da superfície interior. Para reforçar essa sensação, as janelas possuem uma dimensão que permite a entrada de luz natural a qualquer hora do dia. O terraço está limitado, por um lado, por painéis de madeira; pelo outro, uma orla de canas secas e canas de bambu decorativas isolam-no dos vizinhos.

En glasdörr möjliggör tillträde till terrassen, och gör därmed att bostadsytan inomhus känns större. Därav också storleken på fönstren, som släpper in ljuset oavsett tidpunkt på dagen. På ena sidan har terrassens yta begränsats av träpaneler, på andra sidan avskiljs den från grannarna med hjälp av torra vassrör och dekorativ bambu.

TERRACE AND GARDEN

The architects improved the original roof structure of this garden atop a New York building which presented a combination of irregular levels and reconfigured the geometry of the view. The cedar wall on three of the four sides was designed to reflect the horizontal details visible on neighboring buildings. Horizontal firwood crossbeams designed like a trellis were added to obtain shade.

Les architectes ont amélioré la structure d'origine du toit de ce jardin en haut d'un bâtiment de New York, qui présentait une combinaison de niveaux irréguliers, et ils ont reconfiguré la géométrie de la vue. Le bardage en cèdre, sur trois des quatre côtés, a été conçu pour refléter les détails horizontaux vus sur des bâtiments environnants. Pour avoir de l'ombre, des traverses horizontales en sapin, conçues comme un grillage, ont été ajoutées.

Bei der Begrünung dieses Dachs auf einem hohen Gebäude in New York haben die Architekten die vorhandene Anlage umgestaltet, vor allem die Niveauunterschiede ausgeglichen und den Gesamteindruck verbessert. Die Zedernholzwände auf drei Seiten der Terrasse nehmen optisch die horizontalen Elemente der umliegenden Gebäude auf. Die wie ein Gitter quer gelegten Fichtenholzbalken spenden Schatten.

De architecten verbeterden de oorspronkelijke structuur van deze daktuin in New York die hoogteverschillen vertoonde. Ze gaven de geometrie van het uitzicht opnieuw vorm. De afsluiting van ceder aan drie zijden werd ontworpen als een weerspiegeling van de horizontale details van de omringende gebouwen. Om schaduw te creëren werden horizontale dwarslatten van sparrenhout aangebracht.

Los arquitectos mejoraron la estructura original del tejado de este jardín en lo alto de un edificio de Nueva York, que presentaba una combinación de niveles irregulares, y reconfiguraron la geometría de la vista. El cerramiento de cedro, en tres de los cuatro laterales, reproduce las franjas horizontales de los edificios circundantes. Para obtener sombra, se añadieron travesaños de abeto horizontales, diseñados como un enrejado.

L'intervento ha migliorato la struttura originale del tetto di un edificio di New York, che presentava livelli irregolari, e ne ha riconfigurato la composizione geometrica. Il recinto di cedro, su tre lati, è stato concepito in modo da richiamare i dettagli orizzontali che si vedono in edifici circostanti. Per l'ombra, sono state aggiunte traverse di abete, disposte a formare una griglia.

Os arquitectos melhoraram a estrutura original, que apresentava uma combinação de níveis irregulares, e reconfiguraram o enquadramento da paisagem neste jardim no cimo de um edifício de Nova Iorque. A cercadura de cedro, em três dos quatro lados, foi projectada para reproduzir o detalhe das linhas horizontais dos edifícios vizinhos. Para haver sombra, acrescentaram vigas de abeto, a formar um desenho de uma rede.

Arkitekterna förbättrade den här trädgårdens ursprungliga takkonstruktion, högt upp i en byggnad i New York, som var en kombination av oregelbundna nivåer, och utsikten förändrades. Staketet av cederträ, på tre av fyra sidor, skapades för att återspegla de horisontella detaljerna på de kringliggande byggnaderna. För att få skugga lade man ett rutnät av granribbor.

Work was done on this diaphanous flat roof to landscape it and create a multifunctional space: a solarium by day and a place to hold soirees at night. The unique feature of the project lies in the use of autochthonous plant species. The grass carpets that emerge from the Ipe timber flooring, the pomegranates, aromatic plants, and cardboard palms are characterized by their resistance to the harsh conditions of an open-air urban terrace.

Cette terrasse ouverte a été modifiée en ajoutant un jardin et en créant un espace multifonctionnel : un solarium de jour et un lieu pour célébrer une fête la nuit. La singularité de ce projet réside dans l'utilisation d'espèces végétales autochtones. Les tapis de graminées qui sortent du plancher en bois d'ipé, les grenadiers, les plantes aromatiques et le cycas se caractérisent par leur résistance aux dures conditions d'une terrasse urbaine découverte.

Hier wurde eine Dachterrasse in einen Mehrzweckbereich umgewandelt: Am Tag kann man sich entspannt sonnen, am Abend unter freiem Himmel Feste feiern. Der Entwurf besticht durch die Verwendung einheimischer Pflanzen. Der Grasteppich neben dem Deck aus Ipe-Holz, Granatäpfelbäume, Palmfarne und Gewürzkräuter widerstehen den harten Klimabedingungen einer solchen in der Stadt gelegen Terrasse besonders gut.

Van dit lichtdoorlatende dakterras werd een tuin en multifunctionele ruimte gemaakt: een zonneterras voor overdag en een feestlocatie 's avonds. Het bijzondere van dit ontwerp ligt in het gebruik van inheemse planten. De grastapijten onder de verhoging van ipéhout, de granaatappelbomen, de aromatische planten en de varenpalm zijn bestand tegen de barre weersomstandigheden van een stedelijk terras.

Se intervino en esta diáfana azotea para ajardinarla y crear un espacio multifuncional: solárium de día y un lugar donde celebrar una fiesta de noche. La singularidad de este proyecto reside en la utilización de especies vegetales autóctonas. Las alfombras de gramíneas que salen de la tarima de madera de ipé, los granados, las plantas aromáticas y la cica se caracterizan por su resistencia a las duras condiciones de una terraza urbana al descubierto.

Su questo diafano lastrico solare è stato creato uno spazio polifunzionale verde: solarium di giorno e luogo per feste di notte. La particolarità di questo progetto risiede nell'uso di specie vegetali autoctone. I tappeti di graminacee che escono dall'assito di legno di ipè, i melograni, le piante aromatiche e i cycas sono specie molto resistenti alle dure condizioni di una terrazza urbana scoperta.

Com a intervenção sobre esta açoteia, pretendeu-se criar um jardim e um espaço multifuncional: um solário durante o dia que pudesse transformar-se em lugar de festa à noite. A singularidade deste projecto reside na utilização de espécies vegetais autóctones. Os tapetes de gramíneas que brotam de paletes de madeira de ipé, as romãzeiras, as plantas aromáticas e a cica têm em comum a resistência às condições agrestes de um terraço urbano.

Den här ljusa takterrassen gjordes om för att skapa en trädgård och ett multifunktionellt utrymme: solarium under dagen och festlokal på kvällen. Det ovanliga med projektet är de inhemska växtarterna. Gräsliknande mattor på golvet av ipe- trä, granatäppleträden, kryddväxterna och cykadéer kännetecknas av sin motståndskraft mot de svåra förhållandena som väntar på en urban terrass utan tak.

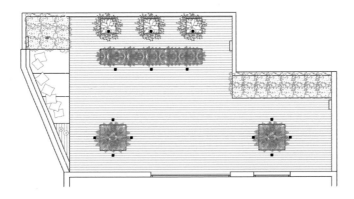

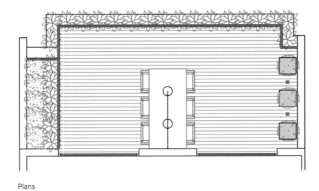

Plans

Work was done on the terrace of this city penthouse loft to create continuity between the interior living room and the outdoors with Ipe timber flooring surrounded by marble balls. A robust timber pergola shields the small living and dining rooms. Access to the solarium is via a wooden walkway where a shower was installed. The wall with dyed pine fences and the landscaped areas around the outside shore up the unity.

Sur la terrasse de ce loft situé au dernier étage d'un immeuble, l'objectif a consisté à créer une continuité entre la zone du living à l'intérieur et l'extérieur par l'intermédiaire d'une estrade en ipé entourée de galets en marbre. Une solide pergola en bois protège le petit salon et la salle à manger. L'accès au solarium s'effectue par une passerelle en bois sur laquelle a été installée une douche. Le mur avec des barrières en pin teint et le jardin périphérique renforcent l'unité.

Diese Terrasse gehört zu einem Penthouse in einem Stadtgebäude. Dem Wunsch nach einem fließenden Übergang vom Wohnraum hinaus wurde durch einen Ipe-Holz-Steg über einem Marmorkieselbett entsprochen. Eine robuste Pergola aus Holz schützt Sitzecke und Essplatz. Ein Holzsteg führt zur Sonnenterrasse mit Dusche. Eine Wand aus getönter Kiefer mit umlaufenden Pflanzkästen verleiht der Anlage Geschlossenheit.

Op dit terras bij een penthouse in de stad moest de woonkamer overgaan in de buitenruimte door de aanleg van een vloer van ipéhout omzoomd met marmersteentjes. Een stevige houten pergola zorgt voor beschutting in de zit- en eethoek. Een houten loopplank leidt naar het zonneterras met douche. Door de muur met een afrastering van geverfd vurenhout en het groen rondom wordt alles meer tot een geheel.

En la terraza de este *loft* ubicado en un sobreático urbano, el objetivo fue crear una continuidad entre la zona del *living* del interior con el exterior mediante una tarima de ipé rodeada por bolos de mármol. Una robusta pérgola de madera resguarda el pequeño salón y el comedor. Una pasarela de madera lleva al solárium, equipado con una ducha. El muro con vallas de pino teñido y la jardinería perimetral refuerzan la unidad.

Sulla terrazza di questo *loft* di un superattico urbano, il fine è stato creare una continuità tra la zona interna del *living* e l'esterno, mediante un assito di ipè circondato da bocce di marmo. Una pergola di legno ripara la piccola zona pranzo. Al solarium si accede per mezzo di una passerella di legno con doccia. La sensazione di unità è rafforzata dai recinti di pino e dal giardino perimetrale.

No terraço deste *loft,* que ocupa um sótão urbano, pretendeu-se criar uma continuidade entre a zona do *living* no interior e o exterior, através de um estrado de ipé rodeado por colunas de mármore. Uma robusta pérgula de madeira protege a sala e a área de jantar. Uma passadeira de madeira dá acesso ao solário onde existe um chuveiro. A parede formada por uma cerca em pinho eo jardim ao longo do perímetro reforçam a unidade.

På terrassen till detta loft, i en takvåning i staden, var målet att skapa kontinuitet mellan vardagsrummet inomhus och exteriören genom en upphöjning i ipe- trä omgiven av marmorklot. En robust pergola i trä skyddar det lilla vardagsrummet och matsalen. Man når solariet via en gångbro av trä där en dusch placerats. Väggen med staket i färgad furu och växterna runtomkring förstärker enheten.

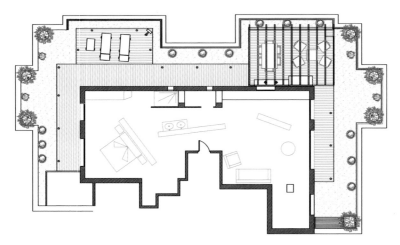

Plan

CHILL OUT AND **SOLARIUM**

ARBORÈTUM
www.arboretum.es
© Jordi Jové

This project is a demonstration of a very ornate chillout space with solarium. Set on the upper floor of a duplex apartment and accessed via a studio, an aluminum pergola covered with an awning and side screens delimits the zone that features a u-shaped sofa to encourage guests to mingle. In front, a landscaped solarium with a pair of beach chairs brings a new use to the place.

Ce projet présente la réalisation d'un *chill out* très complet avec solarium. Il s'agit du deuxième étage d'un duplex auquel on accède par un bureau. Une pergola avec une structure en aluminium, recouverte d'un auvent et de *screens* latéraux, délimite la zone de réunion composée d'un canapé en U favorisant la communication entre les usagers. Devant, un solarium aménagé en espace vert avec deux chaises longues confère un autre usage à cet espace.

Im Rahmen dieses Projekts wurde ein kompletter Chill-out-Bereich mit Sonnenterrasse angelegt. Die Terrasse befindet sich in der zweiten Etage einer Maisonnette und ist über ein Atelier zu erreichen. Eine Alu-Pergola mit Dach aus Segeltuch und seitlichen Zeltbahnen rahmt den Sitzbereich ein, wo ein Sofa in U-Form zum Plaudern einlädt, während auf der begrünten Terrasse Liegestühle zum Sonnen bereit stehen.

Dit ontwerp toont een zeer complete relaxruimte met zonneterras. Het betreft de verdieping van een duplexwoning, die via een studio te betreden is. Een aluminium pergola, overdekt met een zonnescherm en schuttingdelen opzij, schermt de ruimte af met de U-vormige bank die uitnodigt tot conversatie. Daarvóór vervult het zonneterras met beplanting en enkele ligstoelen nog een extra functie.

Este proyecto muestra la realización de un *chill out* muy completo con solárium. Se trata de la segunda planta de un dúplex, a la que se accede a través de un estudio. Una pérgola con estructura de aluminio, cubierta con un toldo y *screens* laterales, delimita la zona de reunión, compuesta por un sofá en forma de U que favorece la comunicación. Delante, un solárium ajardinado con un par de tumbonas proporciona un nuevo uso a este espacio.

Il progetto è quello di un *chill out* con solarium. Si tratta del secondo piano di un duplex, cui si accede attraverso uno studio. Una pergola con struttura d'alluminio, coperta con un telo e *screens* laterali, delimita la zona salotto composta da un sofà a U che favorisce la comunicazione. Davanti a questa, un solarium con giardino e sdraio dà a questo luogo una nuova funzione.

Este projecto mostra a realização de um *chill out* muito completo, com solário. Trata-se do segundo piso de um duplex, com acesso através de um estúdio. Uma pérgula em estrutura de alumínio, coberta com um toldo e telas laterais, delimita a zona de convívio composta por um sofá em U para favorecer a comunicação entre os convivas. Na frente, um solário ajardinado, com duas espreguiçadeiras, permite tirar outro partido do espaço.

Det här projektet visar hur ett fulländat "chill out"- rum med solarium har skapats. Det rör sig om andra våningen i en etagevåning, som man når genom arbetsrummet. En pergola i aluminium, med soltak och skärmar, avgränsar mötesplatsen – en u-formad soffa som minskar avstånden mellan dem som använder den. Framtill får utrymmet en ny funktion genom ett solarium med trädgård och ett par vilstolar.

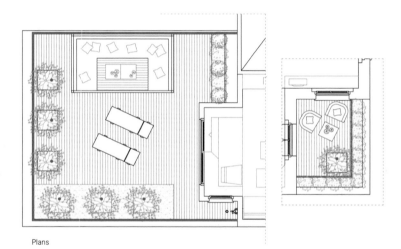

Plans

Large diamond-shaped lattices, a table with a mosaic-tile top, bamboo curtains, a fountain, and candles define this space with an Arabic feel. The summer dining area sits beneath a timber pergola with a wavy canvas top and roll-up wicker curtains. To the right, a service area has been closed off with a pair of mobile lattice frames where a custom-made fountain was installed.

Des treillages maille losange, une table recouverte de mosaïque en céramique, des rideaux en roseau, une fontaine et des bougies définissent cet espace avec des réminiscences arabes. La table pour manger l'été se situe sous une pergola en bois recouverte d'une toile ondulée et des rideaux en osier enroulables. À sa droite, une zone de service a été fermée avec deux treillages mobiles entre lesquels une fontaine sur mesure a été installée.

Hölzerne Scherengitter als Trennwände, ein Tisch mit Keramikmosaik, Vorhänge aus Schilfrohr, ein Brunnen und dazu Kerzenlicht – entstanden ist ein Raum mit maurischen Anklängen. Der Sommeressplatz befindet sich unter einer Pergola mit raffbarem Zeltdach und seitlich angebrachten Schilfrohrrollos. Der daneben liegende Wirtschaftsbereich bleibt hinter Stellwänden und einem Springbrunnen verborgen.

Een ruitvormig latwerk, een tafel met een blad van keramisch mozaïek, jaloezieën van riet, een fontein en kaarsen bepalen de enigszins oosterse sfeer in deze ruimte. De eethoek staat onder een houten pergola met een dak van geplooid canvas en rieten rolgordijnen. Rechts daarvan is een zone met voorzieningen afgeschermd door jaloezieën waartussen een op maat gemaakte fontein is geïnstalleerd.

Celosías de rombo abierto, mesa con sobre de mosaico cerámico, cortinas de caña, una fuente y velas definen este espacio con reminiscencias árabes. El comedor de verano se ubica bajo una pérgola de madera con techo de lona en ondas y cortinas de mimbre enrollables. A su derecha, se ha cerrado una zona de servicios con un par de celosías móviles entre las que se instaló una fuente diseñada a medida.

Gelosie a rombi, tavolo con piano di mosaico ceramico, tende di canna, una fontana e delle candele definiscono questo spazio con reminiscenze arabe. La zona pranzo estiva sta sotto una pergola di legno con soffitto di telo a onde e tende avvolgibili di vimini. Alla sua destra, è stata chiusa un'area di servizi con un paio di gelosie mobili tra le quali è stata installata una fontana fatta su misura.

Persianas de losango aberto, mesa com tampo de mosaico, cortinas de bambu, uma fonte e velas emprestam a este espaço reminiscências árabes. As refeições no Verão têm lugar sob uma pérgula de madeira com tecto de lona ondulado e estores de vime enroláveis. À direita, foi criada uma zona de serviço, fechada com persianas móveis entre as quais se instalou uma fonte feita à medida.

Rutmönstrade jalusier, bord med yta av keramisk mosaik, bambugardiner, en fontän och ljus ger det här utrymmet en arabisk prägel. Sommarmatrummet återfinns under en träpergola med tak av kanvas och flätade rullgardiner. Till höger har man avskiljt ett toalettområde med hjälp av ett par flyttbara jalusier mellan vilka en skräddarsydd fontän placerats.

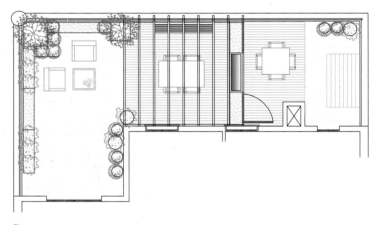

Plan

FLOWER AND FRUIT GARDEN ON THE ROOF

ARBORÈTUM
www.arboretum.es
© Jordi Jové

This garden is located on the flat roof of a contemporary-style property close to the sea. The timber window boxes alternate with terracotta pot plants in which leafy Mediterranean species grow. An arbor communicates the house below with the roof that is divided into two areas: the solarium with a shower and summer dining area, with furniture that boasts an aluminum structure and timber bodies, and a parasol with an articulated arm.

Ce verger se situe sur la terrasse d'une maison de style moderne, près de la mer. Les jardinières en bois alternent avec des pots en terre cuite où poussent des espèces luxuriantes d'essence méditerranéenne. Une tonnelle relie la maison, en bas, à cette terrasse, divisée en deux zones : le solarium avec douche et la salle à manger d'été, avec du mobilier en aluminium et en bois, ainsi qu'un parasol avec un bras articulé.

Dieser Garten liegt auf dem Dach eines modernen Gebäudes nahe der Küste. In hölzernen Pflanzkübeln und Töpfen aus Terrakotta gedeihen typisch mediterrane Gewächse. Über einen Pavillon sind die darunter liegende Wohnung und die Terrasse miteinander verbunden. Die Dachterrasse gliedert sich in Sonnendeck, Dusche und Sommeressplatz mit Möbeln aus Aluminium und Holz unter einem großen Sonnenschirm.

Deze tuin bevindt zich op het dakterras van een moderne woning vlak aan zee. De houten plantenbakken worden afgewisseld met terracotta bloempotten beplant met weelderig, mediterraan groen. Een prieel verbindt de woning beneden met dit in twee zones verdeelde dakterras (zonneterras met douche en eetgedeelte met meubilair met aluminium frame en houten zitting, en een parasol op verstelbare poot).

Este vergel se sitúa en la azotea de una vivienda de estilo moderno, cerca del mar. Las jardineras de madera se alternan con macetas de terracota en las que crecen frondosas especies de esencia mediterránea. Una glorieta comunica la vivienda, abajo, con esta azotea dividida en dos zonas: el solárium, con ducha, y el comedor de verano, con mobiliario de estructura de aluminio y cuerpos de madera, y un parasol de brazo articulado.

Il giardino è situato sul lastrico solare di una casa moderna vicina al mare. Le fioriere di legno sono alternate a vasi di terracotta nei quali crescono specie di latifoglie d'essenza mediterranea. Una pergola mette in comunicazione la casa, di sotto, con questa terrazza divisa in due zone: il solarium, con doccia, e l'area pranzo estiva, arredata con mobili di struttura d'alluminio e corpo di legno, e un parasole con braccio articolato.

Este pomar situa-se na açoteia de uma vivenda moderna, perto do mar. As floreiras em madeira alternam-se com potes de terracota em que crescem frondosas espécies de aromas mediterrânicos. Um pequeno caramanchão comunica a vivenda, em baixo, com a açoteia dividida em duas zonas: o solário, com duche, e o espaço para refeições no Verão, com mobiliário com estrutura de alumínio e corpos de madeira, e um guarda-sol de pé articulado.

Den här trädgården ligger på takterrassen i en bostad i modern stil, nära havet. Blomlådorna av trä kombineras med terrakottakrukor med frodiga växtarter från medelhavet. En berså kopplar samman bostadens nedre del med takterrassen som delats upp i två utrymmen: solariet med dusch och sommarmatsalen, med möbler med aluminiumstruktur och trästomme, samt solskydd.

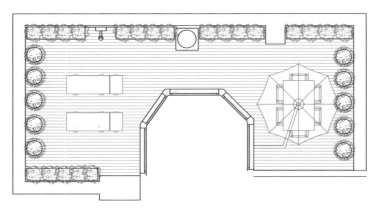

Plan

This spacious terrace surrounds the front part a first-floor urban building and juts out over a busy street. Recovering it brought new meaning to this privileged space. Structures made from Ipe timber boards were built around the edges for protection from curious passersby and to integrate the terrace in the home. A number of large plant pots were positioned, containing hefty trees and aromatic plants.

Cette vaste terrasse entoure la partie avant du premier étage d'un bâtiment urbain et donne sur une promenade fréquentée. La rénovation de cet espace privilégié lui a donné un nouveau sens. Pour se protéger des regards curieux et intégrer la terrasse à la maison, des structures réalisées avec des lattes de bois d'ipé ont été élevées à la périphérie. Des jardinières, dans lesquelles ont été plantés de grands arbres et des plantes aromatiques, ont été installées.

Diese großzügige Terrasse liegt an der Vorderseite eines Stadthauses, direkt über einer viel befahrenen Straße. Bei der Umgestaltung wurde daher besonderer Wert auf die Abschirmung nach außen und die Verbindung von Terrasse und Wohnraum gelegt. Jetzt schützt die hohe Umfassung aus Ipe-Holz vor neugierigen Blicken. Davor stehen Pflanzkübel mit Gewürzpflanzen und großen Bäumen.

Dit ruime terras ligt rondom het voorste gedeelte van de eerste verdieping van een gebouw boven een drukke promenade. Bij de herinrichting kreeg deze prachtig gelegen ruimte een nieuwe functie. Om geen last te hebben van nieuwsgierige blikken en het terras in de woning te integreren, werd rondom een structuur van ipéhout aangebracht. In de bloembakken staan bomen en aromatische planten.

Esta amplia terraza rodea la parte anterior del primer piso de un edificio urbano y se asoma a un concurrido paseo. La reforma ha dado un nuevo sentido a este espacio privilegiado. Para resguardarse de las miradas curiosas e integrar la terraza en la vivienda, se levantaron perimetralmente unas estructuras realizadas con listones de madera de ipé. Se colocaron unas jardineras en las que se plantaron grandes árboles y plantas aromáticas.

In questo caso, la terrazza circonda la parte anteriore del primo piano di un edificio urbano e si sporge su un corso sempre affollato. Grazie all'intervento di ristrutturazione, le è stato dato un nuovo senso. Per evitare gli sguardi curiosi e unire la terrazza alla casa, sono state poste alcune strutture perimetrali fatte di listelli di legno di ipè, oltre a fioriere con grandi alberi e piante aromatiche.

Este amplo terraço rodeia a parte anterior do primeiro piso de um prédio urbano virado para um passeio muito frequentado. Com a recuperação, este espaço adquiriu um novo sentido, ficando resguardado de olhares curiosos – através da colocação de umas ripas verticais de madeira de ipé – e integrado na zona de habitação. Foram ainda colocados vasos com árvores grandes e plantas aromáticas.

Den här breda terrassen omger den främre delen av en stadsbostads första våning och har utsikt över ett välbesökt promenadstråk. Vid renoveringen gav man det här privilegierade utrymmet en ny mening. För att skydda sig mot nyfikna blickar och koppla samman terrassen med bostaden lät man bygga några ribbkonstruktioner av träslaget ipe. Några blomlådor med stora träd och kryddväxter ställdes dit.

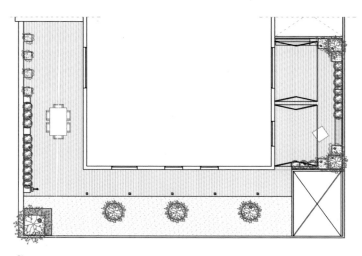

Plan

The terrace of this downtown penthouse is a true garden between tall buildings in which to while away time eating and enjoying the sun. To create privacy, the wall was covered with Ipe timber as a continuation of the pavement, finished with a timber board fence. The dining area spreads beneath a pergola with a glass-covered streaked pine structure that allows light in.

Cette terrasse au dernier étage d'un immeuble du centre-ville possède un véritable jardin au milieu de hauts bâtiments, idéal pour passer des moments agréables, manger et bronzer. Pour plus d'intimité, le mur a été revêtu de bois d'ipé, comme une continuation du sol, et se termine par une barrière de lattes de bois. La salle à manger se situe sous une pergola avec une structure en pin teint et un toit en verre qui laisse entrer la lumière.

Mitten im Stadtzentrum liegt das Dachgeschoss mit dieser Terrasse: ein wirklicher Garten zwischen hohen Gebäuden, gedacht zum Entspannen, zum Sonnen und zum Essen mit Freunden. Die Brüstung wurde wie der Boden mit Brettern aus Ipe-Holz verkleidet und schirmt den Bereich nach außen hin ab. Der Essplatz befindet sich unter einer Pergola aus getöntem Kiefernholz mit lichtdurchlässigem Glasdach.

Dit terras op een bovenverdieping te midden van hoge gebouwen in het centrum van de stad heeft een echte tuin, waar het goed toeven is en waar men kan eten en zonnebaden. Ter wille van de privacy werd de muur met ipéhout bekleed, als een voortzetting van de vloer, en eindigt hij in een hek van latwerk. De eethoek staat onder een pergola van geverfd vurenhout en een lichtdoorlatend glazen dak.

Esta terraza de un ático del centro de la ciudad presenta un auténtico jardín entre edificios altos donde pasar momentos agradables, comer y tomar el sol. Para crear intimidad, se revistió el muro con madera de ipé, como una continuación del pavimento, y se remató con una valla de listones de madera. El comedor se ubica bajo una pérgola con estructura de pino teñido y cubierta de vidrio que permite la entrada de luz.

Questa terrazza di un attico del centro ha un vero e proprio giardino in cui passare qualche gradevole momento, mangiare e prendere il sole. Per una maggiore intimità, il muro è stato rivestito con legno di ipè, come una prosecuzione del pavimento, ed è sormontato da una recinzione di listelli di legno. La zona pranzo si trova sotto una pergola con struttura di pino tinteggiato e vetro per far passare la luce.

Este terraço de um último andar no centro da cidade é um verdadeiro jardim entre edifícios altos onde passar momentos agradáveis, saborear uma refeição ou tomar banhos de sol. A parede foi revestida com madeira de ipé, para dar privacidade, continuidade ao pavimento, rematado com uma cerca de ripas de madeira. A zona para refeições fica sob uma pérgula com estrutura de pinho tingido e coberta de vidro para a entrada da luz.

Den här terrassen tillhörande en vindsvåning i centrum visar en autentisk trädgård mellan höga byggnader där man kan tillbringa trevliga stunder, äta och sola. För att skapa avskildhet har väggen beklätts med ipe- trä, vilket gör att den liknar en förlängning av golvet, och avslutats med ett staket av träribbor. Matsalen finns under en glastäckt pergola i färgad furu, som släpper in ljus.

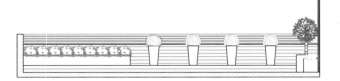

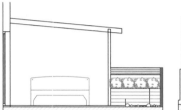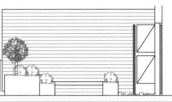

Sections

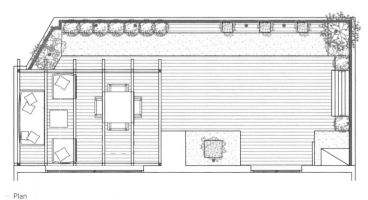

Plan

DOLOMITES HOUSE

JM ARCHITECTURE
www.jma.it
© Gasser; Jacopo Mascheroni

The terrace of this house is closed with an eight-ft-high wall of horizontal timber boards which highlights the perspective and projects the shadows from the sun overhead and the reflectors from below. The house is surrounded by 5.5-inch-wide Ipe timber boards that culminate in a platform for sunbathing, where the jacuzzi is positioned. The floorboards can be covered with a white glass canopy.

La terrasse de cette maison est entourée d'un mur en lattes de bois horizontales de 2,4 m de haut, qui fait ressortir la perspective et projette l'ombre du soleil d'en haut et celle des réflecteurs d'en bas. La maison est entourée d'une estrade en lattes de bois d'ipé de 14 cm de large, qui s'achève sur une plate-forme destinée aux bains de soleil et dotée d'un jacuzzi. Il est possible de recouvrir cette estrade d'une marquise blanche.

Die 2,4 Meter hohe Umfassungsmauer dieser Terrasse ist mit waagerecht angebrachten Holzbrettern verkleidet, die tagsüber Schatten spenden und nachts von unten angestrahlt werden. Das Haus ist von einer Plattform aus 14 cm breiten Ipe-Dielen umgeben, über der sich ein Podest zum Sonnen mit einem Whirlpool erhebt. Dieser Bereich kann mit einem weißen Sonnensegel abgedeckt werden.

Het terras van dit huis wordt omringd door een 2,4 m hoge wand van horizontaal aangebrachte latten die het uitzicht benadrukt en zowel van bovenaf als van onderaf voor schaduw zorgt. Rondom het huis is een verhoging van 14 cm brede ipéhouten planken aangebracht, die eindigt in een platform om te zonnen, met jacuzzi. De verhoging kan worden overdekt met een witte luifel.

El jardín de esta casa, situada en las montañas Dolomitas, está cercado por una pared de listones de madera horizontales de 2,4 m de altura, que resalta la perspectiva y proyecta las sombras del sol desde arriba y de los reflectores desde abajo. La casa está rodeada por una tarima de tablones de madera de ipé de 14 cm de ancho, que acaba con una plataforma para tomar el sol junto al *jacuzzi*.

La terrazza di questa casa è recintata da una parete di listelli di legno orizzontali alti 2,4 m, che accentua la prospettiva e proietta ombre dall'alto, per la luce del sole, e dal basso, per la presenza di riflettori. La casa è circondata da un assito di legno di ipè largo 14 cm, che culmina in una piattaforma con *jacuzzi*. Il tavolato può essere protetto con una tettoia bianca.

O terraço desta casa é rodeado por uma parede de ripas de madeira horizontais de 2,4 m de altura, que destaca a perspectiva e projecta as sombras do sol de cima e dos reflectores de baixo. A casa está rodeada por uma passadeira de tábuas de madeira de ipé de 14 cm de largura, que termina numa plataforma para tomar banhos de sol com *jacuzzi*. A passadeira pode ser coberta com uma protecção branca.

Terrassen på det här huset har avskilts med hjälp av en vägg av 2,4 m höga träribbor som placerats horisontellt och som framhäver perspektivet, samt låter skuggorna avteckna sig från solen uppifrån och från speglarna nerifrån. Huset omges av en upphöjning av 14 cm breda plankor av ipe- trä, som kulminerar i en plattform där man kan sola och bada jacuzzi. Upphöjningen kan täckas med en vit markis.

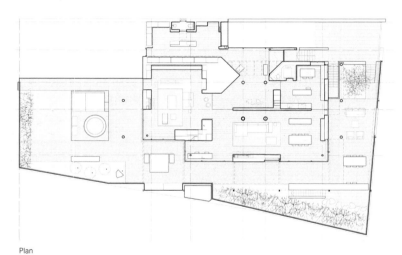

Plan

MATT GIBSON a+d
www.mattgibson.com.au
© John Wheatley

The principal element of this terrace is the fountain at one end, built from a red front panel that runs around the perimeter of the surrounding wall. Floorboards cover a part of the ground and mark a path around the property through to the point where the water flows from the fountain. At night, halogen lights provide enough light to relax at the end of the day.

Le principal élément de cette terrasse est la fontaine située à l'une des extrémités et construite à partir d'une partie frontale rouge, qui parcourt le mur entourant la terrasse. Le plancher en bois couvre une partie du sol et marque le chemin autour de la maison, jusqu'au point où tombe l'eau de la fontaine. Pendant la nuit, des lampes halogènes éclairent suffisamment pour pouvoir se relaxer pendant les dernières heures du jour.

Diese Terrasse wird beherrscht von der Brunnenanlage an einem Ende. Ihr rote Vorderseite setzt sich entlang der Umfassungsmauer fort. Ein Teil des Bodens ist mit Holzdielen ausgelegt und gibt den Weg vor, der einen um das Haus herum bis zum Brunnen führt. Am Abend bzw. in der Nacht sorgen Halogenstrahler für die nötige Beleuchtung, um den Tag entspannt ausklingen zu lassen.

Het belangrijkste object van dit terras is de fontein aan een van de uiteinden, die gemaakt is met het rood in de omringende muur als uitgangspunt. De plankenvloer bedekt deels de grond en geeft het loopgedeelte rond het huis aan tot het punt waar het water uit de fontein komt. 's Avonds zorgen halogeenlampen voor het nodige licht om ook in de late uurtjes te kunnen ontspannen.

El principal elemento de esta terraza es la fuente situada en uno de los extremos, construida a partir de un frontal rojo que recorre el perímetro del muro circundante. El suelo de madera entarimada cubre parte del suelo y marca el recorrido alrededor de la casa hasta el punto donde cae el agua de la fuente. Durante la noche, unas luces halógenas aportan la iluminación necesaria para poder relajarse en las últimas horas del día.

L'elemento principale di questa terrazza è la fontana, costruita su una parete frontale rossa che segue il perimetro del muro esterno. Il pavimento è parzialmente rivestito di parquet che segna il percorso intorno alla casa fino al punto in cui cade l'acqua della fontana. Alcune lampade alogene danno la luce necessaria per godersi un momento di relax nelle ultime ore della giornata.

O elemento principal deste terraço é a fonte situada num dos extremos e construída a partir de um frontal vermelho que percorre todo o perímetro de parede circundante. O caminho em redor da casa é composto por um pavimento de madeira até à queda da água da fonte. Para a noite, foram instaladas umas luzes halogéneas que derramam a claridade necessária para proporcionar um óptimo descanso nas últimas horas do dia.

Det huvudsakliga inslaget på den här terrassen är fontänen vid en av ytterkanterna, som skapats utifrån den röda panelen på väggen. Parketten täcker en del av golvet och markerar en väg runt huset till den plats där fontänens vatten rinner ut. På natten ger några halogenlampor tillräckligt ljus för att man ska kunna slappna av under dygnets sista timmar.

ARBORÈTUM
www.arboretum.es
© Jordi Jové

This hotel has a terrace exclusively for guests to relax on. While they bathe or get a message they can relax and enjoy the sea views. Three pinewood pergolas were built to protect the spa area, massage beds and three relaxing showers.

Cet hôtel dispose d'une terrasse réservée à la détente des clients. Ils peuvent se délecter de la vue sur la mer tout en se baignant ou en se faisant masser. Trois pergolas en bois de pin ont été construites pour protéger l'espace du spa, les tables de massage et les trois douches relaxantes.

Dieses Hotel verfügt über eine Terrasse, die ausschließlich der Erholung der Gäste vorbehalten ist. Während man entspannt badet oder sich massieren lässt, kann man den Blick auf das Meer genießen. Es wurden drei Pergolen aus Pinienholz errichtet, um den Spa-Bereich, die Massageliegen und die Relax-Duschen zu beschirmen.

Dit terras is uitsluitend bedoeld als ontspanningsruimte voor de gasten van het hotel. Wanneer ze zwemmen of zich laten masseren, werkt het uitzicht op zee ontspannend. Er werden drie grenenhouten pergola's gebouwd die bescherming bieden tegen de zon in het spa-gedeelte, op de massagebedden en de in drie douches.

Este hotel dispone de una terraza exclusiva para el relax de sus huéspedes, que pueden disfrutar de las vistas al mar mientras se bañan o reciben un masaje. Se construyeron tres pérgolas de madera de pino para proteger la zona del *spa,* las camas de masaje y las tres duchas relajantes.

Questo albergo possiede una terrazza esclusiva per il riposo dei suoi clienti. Mentre fanno un bagno o ricevono un massaggio, possono rilassarsi contemplando il mare. Sono state costruite tre pergole di legno di pino per proteggere la zona dello *spa,* i lettini per i massaggi e le tre docce rilassanti.

Este hotel dispõe de uma zona aberta privativa virada para o mar para proporcionar momentos de descontracção aos seus hóspedes, que se podem deleitar contemplando uma vista extraordinária, enquanto se refrescam na piscina ou recebem uma massagem. Foram construídas três pérgulas de madeira de pinho para proteger a zona do *spa,* as camas de massagem e os três duches relaxantes.

På det här hotellet finns en exklusiv terrass där gästerna kan slappna av. Samtidigt som de tar ett bad eller avnjuter massage kan de betrakta utsikten över havet. Tre pergolor i furu byggdes för att skydda spa- avdelningen, massagebänkarna och de tre ytorna där man kan ta en avslappnande dusch.

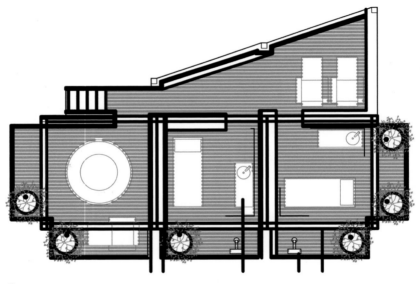

Plan

This luxurious terrace runs the length of the apartment. Gray WPC was used for the surrounding fence. All the rooms in the home open onto this area, considered the most important. Different plants were strategically placed and their position at the sides of the windows of each room means they can be seen from inside.

Cette luxueuse terrasse s'étend sur toute la longueur de l'appartement. Du WPC gris a été utilisé pour la clôture et toutes les pièces de l'appartement donnent sur cet espace, considéré comme le plus important. Diverses plantes ont été placées de manière stratégique ; situées près des fenêtres de chaque pièce, elles peuvent être vues de l'intérieur.

Diese luxuriöse Terrasse erstreckt sich über die Gesamtlänge der Fassade des Appartements. Für die Umfassungswand wurden graue WPC-Bretter (Kunststoff-Holz-Verbund) verwendet. Alle Räume der Wohnung öffnen sich zu diesem Außenbereich hin. Ausgewählte Pflanzen wurden so neben die Fenster der Zimmer platziert, dass sie auch aus dem Inneren der Wohnung zu sehen sind.

Dit terras loopt langs de lengte van het appartement. Voor de omheining werd grijs WPC gebruikt. Alle vertrekken kijken uit op het terras, dat als de belangrijkste ruimte wordt gezien. Op strategische punten staan verschillende planten naast de ramen van alle kamers, waardoor ze ook vanuit het interieur te zien zijn.

Esta lujosa terraza se extiende a lo largo de todo el apartamento. Se usó WPC gris para la cerca que envuelve la terraza. Todas las estancias de la vivienda se abren a esta zona, considerada la más importante. Se colocaron diferentes plantas estratégicamente; su posición al lado de las ventanas de cada habitación permite que se puedan ver desde el interior.

Questa sontuosa terrazza scorre lungo tutto l'appartamento. Per la recinzione è stato usato legno tecnico WPC di colore grigio. Tutti gli ambienti della casa danno su questa zona, che è considerata la più importante. Sono state poste diverse piante in punti strategici, accanto alle finestre di ogni stanza, così che possano essere viste dall'interno.

Este terraço de luxo acompanha a área total do apartamento. Na cerca que envolve o perímetro do terraço, foi usado WPC cinzento. Todas as dependências da vivenda dão para esta área, considerada a mais importante. Foram colocadas várias plantas em posição estratégica com o objectivo de poderem ser vistas do interior de cada quarto.

Den här lyx- terrassen sträcker ut sig över hela lägenheten. Man använde grå trä/plastkomposit (WPC) till staketet runt terrassen. Alla rummen i bostaden öppnar sig mot denna yta, som anses vara det huvudsakliga utrymmet. Växterna syns inifrån eftersom de strategiskt placerades ut bredvid fönstren vid varje rum.

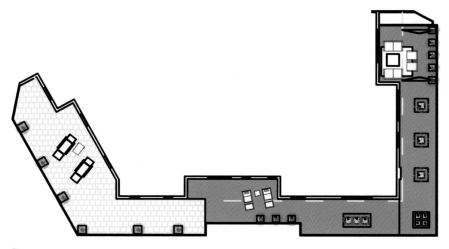

Plan

The terrace of this home comprises three very clearly differentiated areas, each with different uses: a solarium, a dining area and an outdoor living area. The living area is formed of a porch made from a walnut structure, while the dining space has a similar pergola but with a folding polyester roof.

La terrasse de ce logement se compose de trois zones bien distinctes, chacune ayant une utilité différente : un solarium, une salle à manger et une pièce à vivre extérieure. La pièce à vivre est constituée d'un porche avec une structure en bois de noyer, alors que la salle à manger dispose d'une pergola similaire mais constituée d'une toiture pliante en polyester.

Diese Terrasse gliedert sich in drei von einander unabhängige Bereiche, die jeweils unterschiedlichen Nutzungen entsprechen: Liegestühle zum Sonnen, Essplatz und Aufenthaltsbereich mit Sitzecke. Während die Sitzgruppe sich unter einem Vordach aus Nussbaumholz befindet, wird der Sommeressplatz von einer Pergola mit einer faltbaren Polyester-Abdeckung geschützt.

Het terras van deze woning bestaat uit drie onderscheiden gedeelten, elk met een eigen functie: een zonneterras, een eetgedeelte en een zithoek. De zithoek wordt gevormd door een overdekt gedeelte met een notenhouten constructie. Het eetgedeelte bezit heeft een inklapbare overkapping van polyester.

La terraza de esta vivienda se compone de tres áreas perfectamente diferenciadas, cada una con usos diferentes: un solárium, un comedor y una zona de estar exterior. La zona de estar está formada por un porche con estructura de madera de nogal, mientras que el espacio del comedor dispone de una pérgola similar pero formada por una cubierta de poliéster plegable.

La terrazza di questa abitazione si compone di tre aree perfettamente distinte, ognuna adibita a differenti finalità: un solarium, una sala da pranzo e un soggiorno esterno. La zona soggiorno è formata da un portico la cui struttura portante è di legno di noce, mentre lo spazio della sala da pranzo possiede una pergola simile, ma costituita da una tettoia di poliestere pieghevole.

O terraço desta residência é composto por três áreas perfeitamente diferenciadas, cada uma destinada a uma utilização diferente: um solário, uma zona para refeições e outra para estar. A zona de estar é formada por um alpendre com estrutura de madeira de nogueira, enquanto a zona para refeições é protegida por uma pérgula semelhante, mas formada por uma cobertura extensível em poliéster.

Terrassen tillhörande den här bostaden utgörs av tre tydligt åtskilda ytor, var och en avsedd för sitt speciella användningsområde: en solterass, ett matrum och en vardagsrumsliknande yta utomhus. Denna yta består av en veranda med konstruktion i valnötsträ, medan ytan med matplats har en liknande pergola fast med tak av hopfällbart polyestertyg.

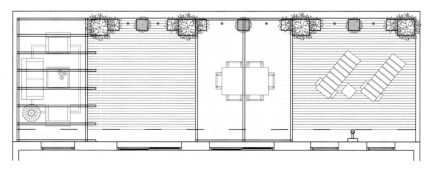

Plan

ARBORÈTUM
www.arboretum.es
© Jordi Jové

This project is located on the ground floor of a property, converted into an urban terrace. A Brazilian tropical walnut platform that runs through to the entrance of the property was built. Of note is an aluminum pergola with a collapsible awning beneath which is the living area.

Ce projet concerne le rez-de-chaussée d'une maison, converti en une terrasse urbaine. Un parquet en noyer tropical brésilien s'étend jusqu'à l'entrée de la maison. Une pergola en aluminium et son store pliant abritent le salon.

Hier handelt es sich um ein Projekt, bei dem vor dem Erdgeschoss eines Einfamilienhauses eine großzügige Terrasse angelegt wurde. Eine Plattform aus tropischen Nussbaumholz aus Brasilien reicht bis an den Eingang der Wohnräume. Über dem Aufenthaltsbereich auf einem ähnlich gestalteten Plankendeck spannt sich eine Pergola aus Aluminium mit einem einfahrbaren Sonnensegel.

Dit ontwerp bevindt zich op de begane grond van een woning. Het is een stadsterras geworden. Het platform van Braziliaans tropisch notenhout loopt door tot de ingang van de woning. Opvallend is de aluminium pergola met opvouwbaar zonnescherm waaronder zich de zithoek bevindt.

Este proyecto se ubica en los bajos de una vivienda, convertidos en una terraza urbana. Se construyó una tarima de nogal tropical brasileño que se extiende hasta la entrada. Destaca una pérgola de aluminio con toldo plegable bajo la cual se encuentra la zona de estar.

Questo progetto è situato in una zona al pianterreno di una casa, trasformata in una terrazza urbana. Si è deciso di costruire una piattaforma di noce tropicale del Brasile che va fino all'ingresso. Fa spicco una pergola d'alluminio con telo pieghevole sotto il quale si trova la zona soggiorno.

Este projecto destina-se a uma vivenda, cujo rés-do-chão assumiu as características de um terraço urbano. Colocou-se um pavimento em madeira de nogueira tropical do Brasil, até à entrada na casa. Destaca-se uma pérgula de alumínio com toldo extensível sob a qual se encontra a zona de estar.

Det här projektet återfinns på en bostads bottenvåning, som gjorts om till en urban terrass. Av tropiskt valnötsträ från Brasilien byggde man ett trädäck som sträcker sig till bostadens ingång. Pergolan i aluminium med hopfällbart tak är ett särdrag. Under den finner man vardagsrumsytan.

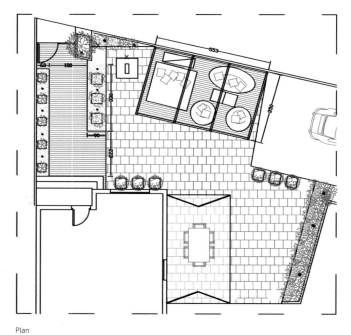

Plan

The patio of this family home was distributed into three differentiated areas: a solarium with a swimming pool; an outdoor dining area and a chill-out space. Although there is not much space, room was found for a pool surrounded by a pinewood platform. A pinewood fence protects the garden from curious strangers.

La cour de cette maison familiale a été divisée en trois zones différentes : un solarium avec piscine, une salle à manger extérieure et un *chill-out*. Malgré les dimensions réduites de la cour, une piscine y a été construite, entourée d'une terrasse en pin. Une clôture, également en pin, protège le jardin des regards indiscrets.

Der Gartenhof dieses Einfamilienhauses wurde in drei Nutzungsbereiche unterteilt: eine Sonnenterrasse mit Schwimmbecken, einen Sommeressplatz und eine Chill-out-Zone. Um das Schwimmbad wurde ein Steg aus behandelten Pinienholzdielen angelegt. Auch die Umfriedung ist aus Pinienholzbrettern und schützt vor neugierigen Blicken.

De patio van deze eengezinswoning werd in drie verschillende zones ingedeeld: een zonneterras met zwembad, een eetgedeelte en een *chill-out*. Ondanks de beperkte afmetingen werd een zwembad aangelegd met daaromheen een platform van grenen latten. Een eveneens grenen omheining biedt de tuin de nodige privacy.

El patio de esta vivienda unifamiliar se distribuyó en tres zonas diferenciadas: un solárium con piscina, un comedor exterior y un *chill-out*. A pesar de las reducidas dimensiones del patio, se construyó una piscina rodeada por una tarima de listones de pino. Una cerca, también de pino, protege el jardín de las miradas ajenas.

Il cortile di questa casa unifamiliare è distribuito in tre zone distinte: un solarium con piscina, una sala da pranzo esterna e un *chill-out*. Nonostante le dimensioni ridotte del cortile, è stata installata una piscina circondata da una piattaforma di listelli di pino. Una recinzione, sempre di pino, protegge il giardino dagli sguardi degli estranei.

O pátio desta vivenda unifamiliar foi distribuído em três zonas distintas: um solário com piscina, uma zona para refeições no exterior e um *chill-out*. Apesar das reduzidas dimensões do pátio, construiu-se uma piscina rodeada por uma superfície de tábuas de pinho. Uma cerca, também de pinho, protege o jardim dos olhares indiscretos.

Den här enfamiljsbostadens patio har delats upp på tre åtskilda ytor: en solterrass med pool, ett uterum med matplats och ett "chill-out"- utrymme. Trots pations lilla yta byggde man en pool som omges av golv i furu. Ett staket, även det av furu, skyddar trädgården mot insyn.

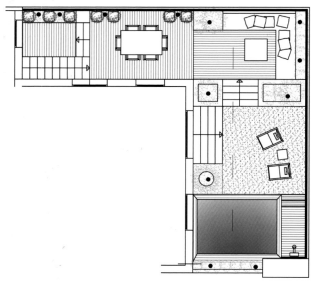

Plan

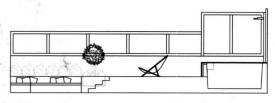

Section

Perspective

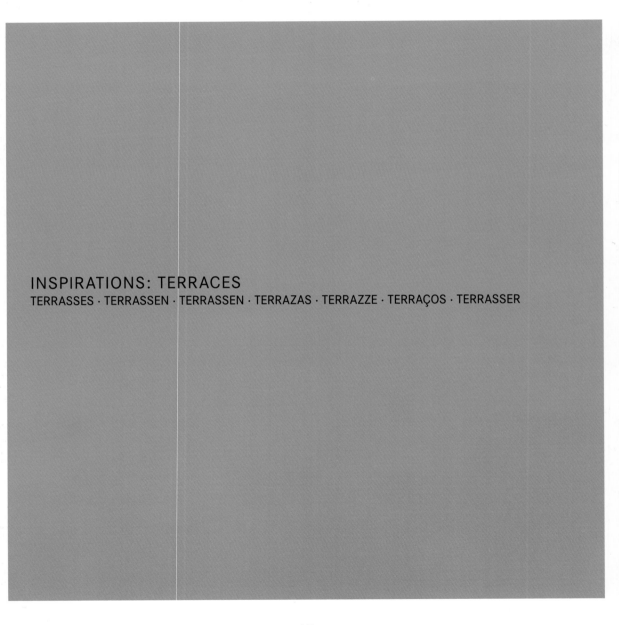

INSPIRATIONS: TERRACES
TERRASSES · TERRASSEN · TERRASSEN · TERRAZAS · TERRAZZE · TERRAÇOS · TERRASSER

BALCONIES

BALCONS · BALKONS · BALKONS · BALCONES · BALCONI · VARANDAS · BALKONGER

Balconies are often wasted spaces of a few square feet which can easily become places to store junk. But if a cozy showcase of plant life is created, the balcony will take on a new life by extending the inside of the property outward. The flooring, materials used in the railings, lattices, pot plants and window boxes, furniture, and plant species will be the components that help make the balcony another inhabitable space.

Les balcons sont généralement des espaces inutilisés, de quelques mètres carrés, qu'il est facile de convertir en débarras. Cependant, la création d'une vitrine accueillante avec une végétation abondante permettra de donner une autre fonction au balcon en prolongeant l'intérieur de la maison vers l'extérieur. Le traitement du sol, les matériaux des rambardes, les treillages, les massifs ou les jardinières, le mobilier et les espèces végétales seront les composants qui contribueront à transformer le balcon en un espace à vivre de plus.

Noch allzu häufig bleiben Balkons ungenutzt, werden oft nur als Abstellräume unter freiem Himmel missbraucht. Doch wenn man aus einem Balkon ein vielfältig begrüntes, ansprechendes Aushängeschild der Wohnung macht, erweitert man zugleich die Wohnfläche nach außen. Bei der Verwandlung dieser wenigen ungenutzten Quadratmeter in einen behaglichen Aufenthaltsraum sind folgende Aspekte besonders zu beachten: der Bodenbelag, das Material der Brüstung, die Jalousien, Markisen oder Trennwände, die Blumentöpfe und Pflanzkästen, die Gartenmöbel und schließlich die Auswahl der Pflanzen.

Van balkons, die meestal maar enkele vierkante meters groot zijn, wordt vaak niet geprofiteerd, waardoor ze de kans lopen te veranderen in een extra opslagruimte. Maar als het balkon aantrekkelijk wordt gemaakt met veel groen, krijgt het een nieuwe functie waardoor de binnenruimte van de woning wordt uitgebreid met plezierige buitenruimte. De afwerking van de vloer, het materiaal van het balkonhek of de balkonwering, een eventueel zonnescherm, de bloempotten en plantenbakken, de tuinmeubels en de gekozen planten zijn de elementen die van een balkon extra woonruimte kunnen maken.

Los balcones suelen ser espacios desaprovechados, de pocos metros cuadrados, que pueden convertirse fácilmente en trasteros. Sin embargo, si se crea un escaparate acogedor y de vegetación abundante, se conseguirá que el balcón adquiera un nuevo uso al prolongar el interior de la vivienda hacia al exterior. El tratamiento del suelo, los materiales de las barandas, las celosías, las macetas y jardineras, el mobiliario y las especies vegetales serán los componentes que ayudarán a convertir el balcón en un espacio habitable más.

I balconi sono di solito spazi sprecati o male usati, di pochi metri quadrati, che possono facilmente finire come ripostigli. Ciò nondimeno, se si crea una vetrina accogliente e con abbondante vegetazione, il balcone svolgerà una nuova funzione prolungando lo spazio abitativo verso all'esterno. Il trattamento del suolo, i materiali delle ringhiere, le gelosie, i vasi e le fioriere, l'arredamento e le specie vegetali saranno i componenti che contribuiranno a trasformare il balcone in una splendida zona della casa.

As varandas são, em regra, espaços desaproveitados, de poucos metros quadrados, que facilmente se convertem lugares de armazenamento. No entanto, se se organizar um escaparate interessante e se decorar com bastantes plantas, conseguir-se-á que a varanda convide a uma nova utilização ao prolongar a residência do interior para o exterior. O tratamento do solo, os materiais de revestimento do chão, as persianas, os vasos e canteiros, o mobiliário e as espécies vegetais serão os elementos que ajudarão a transformar a varanda em mais um espaço para se estar.

Balkonger brukar vara outnyttjade områden, på ett fåtal kvadratmeter, som lätt blir till förrådsutrymmen. Trots detta går det, om man skapar en mysig plats med rikliga mängder växter, att ge balkongen en ny funktion genom att utöka samt lyfta ut bostadens inre. Golvbehandlingen, räckenas material, jalusierna, blomkrukorna och blomlådorna, möblemanget och växtarterna blir komponenter som hjälper till att förvandla balkongen till ytterligare ett beboeligt utrymme.

HOUSE-**BRIDGE**

STANLEY SAITOWITZ/NATOMA ARCHITECTS
www.saitowitz.com
© Rien van Rijthoven

This property occupies six hectares of wooded fields and runs east to west except for a gully that crosses the site. The living areas on the upper floor and the bedrooms have glassed-in walls. The top bridge, protected by a glass-covered balcony, has a platform which is not only used as a dining area but connects the entrance of the house with the paths that lead into the nature.

Cette maison occupe six hectares de prairies boisées et s'étend d'est en ouest, excepté un ravin qui traverse le lieu. Les zones d'habitation du niveau supérieur et les chambres à coucher disposent de baies vitrées. Sur la partie supérieure, protégée par un balcon également vitré, se trouve une plateforme qui, en plus de servir de salle à manger, relie l'entrée de la maison aux sentiers qui pénètrent dans la nature.

Das Anwesen umfasst sechs Hektar waldreiches Weideland und erstreckt sich beiderseits einer Schlucht. Die Wohnräume im Obergeschoss und die Schlafräume verfügen über gläserne Wände. Auf der oberen Plattform mit ihrem verglasten Balkon gibt es einen Bereich, der als Essplatz dient und zugleich den Eingang des Hauses mit den Wegen verbindet, die von hier in die Natur hinaus führen.

Bij dit huis hoort zes hectare bosrijke weidegrond die van west naar oost langs een afgrond loopt. Het woongedeelte op de bovenverdieping en de slaapkamers hebben glazen wanden. Bovenin is een platform dat wordt afgeschermd door een balkon met eveneens glazen wanden. Daar kan worden gegeten en bovendien verbindt het platform de toegang tot het huis met de paden in de omgeving.

Esta casa ocupa seis hectáreas de praderas boscosas y se extiende de este a oeste salvando un barranco que atraviesa el lugar. Las áreas de estar del nivel superior y los dormitorios disponen de paredes acristaladas. En el puente superior, protegido por un balcón también acristalado, hay una plataforma que, además de servir como comedor, conecta la entrada de la casa con los senderos que se adentran en la naturaleza.

Questa casa occupa un'area di sei ettari di praterie boschive e si estende da est a ovest superando perfino un burrone. Le zone giorno del piano superiore e le camere da letto hanno pareti di vetro. Sul ponte superiore, protetta da un balcone anch'esso di vetri, c'è una piattaforma che, oltre a servire da area pranzo, collega l'ingresso della casa con i sentieri che si addentrano nella natura.

Esta casa ocupa seis hectares de prados e bosques e estende-se de Este a Oeste salvando um barranco que atravessa o lugar. As áreas de estar do nível superior e os quartos de dormir dispõem de paredes envidraçadas. Na ponte superior, protegida por uma varanda também envidraçada, há uma plataforma que, além de servir de zona de refeições, liga a entrada da casa com os carreiros que penetram na natureza.

Den här fastigheten upptar sex hektar skogsbevuxen ängsmark och sträcker sig från öst till väst över en dal som går genom platsen. Vardagsrummet på övre plan och sovrummen har glasväggar. Vid den övre bron, som skyddas av en inglasad balkong, finns en plattform som förutom att fungera som matsal kopplar samman husets ingång med de stigar som leder ut i naturen.

ARBORÈTUM
www.arboretum.es
© Jordi Jové

This balcony pertains to a penthouse with exceptional city views. Located in a stately building, the façade has an arbor that makes one end of the balcony truly beautiful, which is why its presence was promoted. The space was designed as a living room for inviting friends. The summer dining area seats ten and a relaxation area was fitted with a buffet and garden.

Ce balcon appartient au dernier étage d'un immeuble avec une vue imprenable sur la ville. Située dans un bâtiment seigneurial, la façade est dotée d'une gloriette, qui confère un caractère exclusif à l'une des extrémités du balcon, dont la présence a été, de ce fait, renforcée. L'espace a été conçu comme une zone d'habitation pour inviter des amis. La salle à manger d'été a une capacité de dix personnes et une zone de repos, avec buffet et jardin, a été aménagée.

Von dem Penthouse, zu dem dieser Balkon gehört, hat man eine herrliche Sicht über die Stadt. Das herrschaftliche Gebäude verfügt über einen repräsentativen Eckturm, der dem Balkon einen eigenen Reiz verleiht. Entstanden ist ein Aufenthaltsbereich für ungezwungene Treffen mit Freunden. Neben dem für zehn Personen ausgelegten Essplatz gibt es einen Barbereich, eine Sitzkombination und einen Garten.

Dit balkon hoort bij een bovenste verdieping met schitterend uitzicht op de stad. In de gevel van het voorname gebouw bevindt zich een prieel dat het balkon aan een van zijn uiteinden iets exclusiefs geeft en dat men daarom extra heeft laten uitkomen. De ruimte is bedoeld om met vrienden te zitten. De eethoek is geschikt voor tien personen en er is een plek met buffet en tuin om te ontspannen.

Este balcón pertenece a un ático con excelentes vistas de la ciudad. Situado en un edificio señorial, la fachada cuenta con una glorieta que otorga exclusividad a uno de los extremos del balcón, por lo que se ha potenciado su presencia. El espacio se concibió como una zona de estar para invitar a los amigos. El comedor de verano cuenta con una capacidad de diez personas y se habilitó un área de descanso con bufé y jardín.

Questo balcone appartiene a un attico di un edificio signorile con eccellente vista sulla città. La sua facciata ha una pergola che dà personalità al balcone, pertanto la sua presenza è stata rafforzata. L'intero spazio è stato concepito come un soggiorno per invitare gli amici. La zona pranzo estiva ha una capienza di dieci persone ed è stata allestita un'area con buffet e giardino.

Esta varanda pertence a um último andar com uma vista excelente da cidade. Encontra-se situado num edifício senhorial, cuja fachada tem um caramanchão muito apelativo numa das extremidades da varanda. O espaço foi concebido como uma zona para receber amigos pelo que a zona de refeições tem lugar para dez pessoas. Além disso, foi criada uma área de descanso com buffet e jardim.

Den här balkongen tillhör en vindsvåning med fantastisk utsikt över staden. På framsidan av detta herrskapshus finns en berså som ger en exklusiv känsla åt balkongens ena sida, vilket gör dess yttre mer kraftfullt. Utrymmet var tänkt som en yta där man kan samlas med sina vänner. Sommarmatsalen har plats för tio personer, och ett viloutrymme med byffé och trädgård skapades.

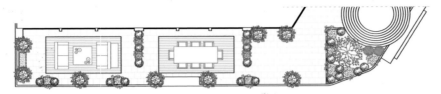

Plan

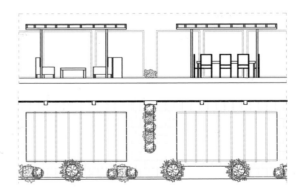

Sections

ARBORÈTUM
www.arboretum.es
© Jordi Jové

On this balcony the idea was to create a welcoming showcase with plenty of plant life. The ground was laid with Ipe flooring and a preliminary row of window boxes and a fountain were built. Set against the balcony wall, a second row of timber pot plants with jungle-inspired vegetation constitutes a curtain of plants, an idea shored up with vertical awnings. An outdoor living area with wicker furniture completes this urban paradise.

L'objectif de ce balcon était de créer une vitrine accueillante avec une végétation abondante. Il a été revêtu de bois d'ipé et une première rangée de jardinières a été installée ainsi qu'une fontaine en dur. Contre le mur du balcon, un second plan de jardinières en bois avec des plantes d'apparence sauvage constitue un véritable rideau végétal, accentué par des auvents verticaux. Un salon extérieur avec du mobilier en osier complète ce paradis urbain.

Der Balkon sollte zu einem freundlichen, üppig begrünten Aushängeschild der Wohnung werden. Der Boden wurde mit Ipe-Holz ausgelegt, eine Reihe Pflanzkübel aufgestellt und ein Springbrunnen gebaut. Die Umfassungsmauer wurde mit weiteren Pflanzkästen ausgestattet, deren dichte Vegetation einen grünen Vorhang bildet, der die Zeltbahnen ergänzt. Die Sitzecke aus Rohrmöbeln macht dieses Paradies perfekt.

Van dit balkon wilde men een prettige ruimte met weelderig groen maken. Er kwamen een vloer van ipéhout, een eerste rij plantenbakken en een fontein. Direct tegen de muur van het balkon kwam rondom een tweede rij houten plantenbakken met boompjes, als een gordijn van groen dat verdicht werd met verticale schermen. De salon in de buitenlucht met rieten meubels completeert dit stedelijke paradijs.

En este balcón se ha buscado la creación de un escaparate acogedor y de vegetación abundante. Se pavimentó con madera de ipé y se construyeron una primera hilera de jardineras y una fuente de obra. Pegado al muro del balcón, un segundo plano perimetral de jardineras de madera con plantas de aspecto selvático constituye una verdadera cortina vegetal que se reforzó con toldos verticales. Un salón exterior con mobiliario de mimbre completa este paraíso urbano.

È stata creata qui un'accogliente vetrina con molta vegetazione e il pavimento, su cui spiccano una fila di fioriere e una fontana di mattoni, è rivestito di ipè. Adiacente al muro del balcone, una seconda serie perimetrale di fioriere di legno con piante dall'aspetto selvatico costituisce una cortina vegetale rafforzata da teli verticali, che racchiude uno splendido salotto esterno con mobili di vimini.

Nesta varanda, procurou-se criar uma zona acolhedora com vegetação frondosa. O pavimento é em madeira de ipé e construiu-se uma fileira de floreiras e uma fonte. Junto à parede da varanda, um segundo plano perimetral de floreiras de madeira com plantas selvagens forma uma espécie de cortina vegetal, que foi reforçada com toldos verticais. Uma sala exterior com mobiliário de bambu completa este paraíso urbano.

På den här balkongen har man försökt skapa en inbjudande plats med riklig växtlighet. Man lade golv av ipe- trä och byggde upp en rad med blomlådor och en fontän. Intill balkongväggen finns fler blomlådor i trä med djungellika växter som bildar ett verkligt draperi av växter, vilket framhävs med vertikala markiser. Ett yttre vardagsrum med korgmöbler fulländar detta paradis i stadsmiljö.

Elevation

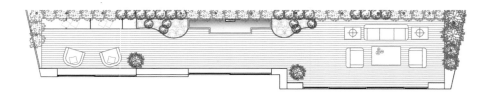

Plan

JORGE HRDINA ARCHITECTS
www.jorgehrdina.com.au
© Eric Sierins

In this coastal house designed by Jorge Hrdina, stone seems to emerge from the weathered escarpment to form the property, as care has been taken to ensure it is hard to distinguish where one starts and the other ends. Pale beige to coppery tones clad the sandstone wall façade which ends with a glassed-in balcony to favor the views of the surroundings.

Dans ce pavillon côtier conçu par Jorge Hrdina, la pierre semble se dresser du terrain escarpé pour former la maison, de telle sorte que l'on ne puisse pas réellement distinguer où commence l'un et où se termine l'autre. Les tons qui vont du beige clair au cuivre accaparent la façade avec des murs en grès, qui s'achève par un balcon vitré afin de favoriser la vue sur l'environnement.

Dieses Chalet an der Küste wurde von Jorge Hrdina entworfen. Ganz bewusst wird hier der Betrachter im Ungewissen darüber gelassen, wo der Felsen aufhört und das Haus anfängt. Helle Beige- und Kupfertöne bestimmen die Fassade aus Sandstein, deren Mauern oben von einem verglasten Balkon abgeschlossen werden, von dem aus man den Blick in die Umgebung genießen kann.

Van dit door Jorge Hrdina ontworpen chalet aan de kust lijkt de steen uit het steile terrein tevoorschijn te komen om de woning te vormen; het is zo ontworpen dat niet goed te zien is waar het een begint en het ander eindigt. De lichtbeige tot koperkleurige tinten slokken de gevel van zandsteen op, die eindigt in een glazen balkon vanwaaraf men van het uitzicht kan genieten.

En este chalé costero diseñado por Jorge Hrdina, la piedra parece erigirse desde dentro del terreno escarpado para formar el edificio, puesto que es difícil distinguir dónde empieza uno y dónde acaba el otro. Los tonos del beis claro al cobrizo acaparan la fachada de muros de arenisca que termina con un balcón acristalado para favorecer las vistas del entorno.

In questa villa costiera, progettata da Jorge Hrdina, la pietra stessa sembra ergersi sul ripido terreno per formare la casa, giacché è stata progettata in modo che non sia possibile distinguere bene dove comincia una finisce l'altra. La facciata di arenaria, con toni che vanno dal beige chiaro al rame, termina con un balcone a vetri per permettere di ammirare il paesaggio.

Nesta casa de praia concebida por Jorge Hrdina, a pedra parece emergir abruptamente do terreno escarpado para dar forma à vivenda. A zona de fronteira entre uma e outra é propositadamente difícil de distinguir. Os tons de bege-claro do alpendre confundem-se com a fachada arenosa que termina numa varanda envidraçada que convida à contemplação da paisagem.

I den här kustvillan, som ritats av Jorge Hrdina, ser det ut som att det kommer ut sten från den branta terrängen, för att utgöra bostaden. Detta eftersom man har strävat efter att gränserna inte ska vara för skarpa. Nyanserna från ljusbeige till kopparfärgat klär sandstensväggen, som avslutas med en inglasad balkong för att framhäva utsikten över omgivningen.

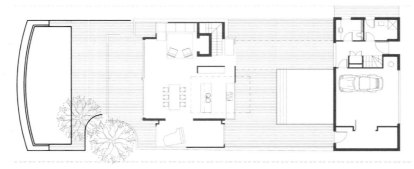

Plan

VILLA **SORAVIA**

COOP HIMMELBLAU
www.coop-himmelblau.at
© Pep Escoda

This luxurious vacation home sits on the shores of Lake Millstatt in Austria. The bottom section is composed of semi-public transparent rooms. The living room boasts enormous floor-to-ceiling windows that enable visual continuity through to the lake via the terrace. A cedar wood pavilion on a raised walkway stands out above the lake.

Cette luxueuse maison de vacances est située au bord du lac Millstatt, en Autriche. La partie inférieure se compose de pièces transparentes semi-publiques. Le salon est doté de grandes baies vitrées, qui occupent toute la hauteur de l'étage et assurent la continuité visuelle jusqu'au lac par l'intermédiaire de la terrasse. Un pavillon en bois de cèdre, situé sur une passerelle élevée, se dresse au-dessus du lac.

Im österreichischen Millstatt steht diese luxuriöse Ferienhaus, in dessen unterem Geschoss sich transparente, von außen einsichtige Räume befinden. Durch die riesigen, bis zur Decke reichenden Fenster des Wohnzimmers kann der Blick hinaus, über die Terrasse hinweg bis zum See schweifen. Auf einem erhöhten Steg erhebt sich dort ein Zedernholzpavillon über dem Wasser.

Dit luxueuze vakantiehuis staat aan de oever van de Millstätter See in Oostenrijk. Het onderste gedeelte bestaat uit halfopen, transparante vertrekken. De woonkamer heeft enorme ramen over de hele hoogte, die via het terras zorgen voor de visuele continuïteit naar het meer. Een verhoogd paviljoen van cederhout steekt boven het meer uit.

Esta lujosa casa de vacaciones está situada a orillas del lago Millstatt, en Austria. La parte inferior está compuesta por habitaciones transparentes semipúblicas. La sala de estar dispone de unos enormes ventanales que ocupan toda la altura de la planta y permiten la continuidad visual hacia el lago a través de la terraza. Un pabellón de madera de cedro situado en una pasarela elevada descuella por encima del lago.

Questa lussuosa casa per le vacanze sorge sulle rive del lago Millstatt, in Austria. La parte inferiore è composta da stanze trasparenti semipubbliche. Il soggiorno ha enormi finestre che arrivano fino al soffitto e permettono una vista panoramica del lago dalla terrazza. Sul lago spicca un padiglione di legno di cedro sito su una passerella elevata.

Esta luxuosa casa de férias fica situada nas margens do lago Millstatt, na Áustria. O andar térreo é formado por divisões transparentes, quase públicas. A sala de estar dispõe de umas janelas enormes que ocupam toda a altura do pé direito e conferem uma continuidade visual até ao lago, através da varanda. Um pavilhão de madeira de cedro situado numa passarela elevada eleva-se sobre o lago.

Den här lyxiga semestervillan ligger strax intill sjön Millstatt, i Österrike. Den nedre delen består av genomskinliga rum, delvis öppna för allmänheten. Vardagsrummet har panoramafönster och möjliggör, genom terrassen, visuell kontinuitet i riktning mot sjön. En paviljong i cederträ på en upphöjd gångbro höjer sig över sjön.

XTEN ARCHITECTURE
www.xtenarchitecture.com
© Art Gray

This home set on a narrow plot in the famous Hollywood Hills integrates with the landscape while also looming over the huge metropolis. All the interior and exterior limits disappear when the front, side and rear elevations open up to connect the internal spaces with the gardens and different-level terraces. It features forty-four sliding glass panels which can be hidden when the occasion requires.

Cette maison enclavée dans un terrain étroit des fameuses collines d'Hollywood est intégrée dans le paysage, tout en donnant sur l'énorme métropole. Toutes les limites d'intérieur et d'extérieur disparaissent lorsque les hauteurs frontales, latérales et arrières s'ouvrent pour relier les espaces internes avec les jardins et les terrasses des niveaux. Elle dispose de quarante-quatre panneaux coulissants en verre, qui peuvent être dissimulés lorsque l'occasion se présente.

Dieses Haus liegt auf einem schmalen Grundstück in den berühmten Hügeln von Hollywood. Es fügt sich gut in die Landschaft ein und bietet doch einen weiten Ausblick über die Metropole. Hier wurde auf einengende Grenzen verzichtet, um die Innenräume ganz zum Garten und den Terrassen auf den jeweiligen Ebenen hin zu öffnen. Die vierundvierzig Glasschiebefenster können bei Bedarf völlig verschwinden.

Dit huis, dat ligt ingeklemd tussen de beroemde heuvels van Hollywood, gaat op in het landschap en kijkt uit op de grote metropool. Alle grenzen binnen en buiten verdwijnen zodra de wanden aan voor, zij- en achterkant geopend worden om de binnenruimten te verbinden met de tuinen en terrassen op de verschillende niveaus. Het huis heeft 44 glazen schuifpanelen die men kan laten verdwijnen.

Esta casa enclavada en un terreno angosto de las famosas colinas de Hollywood se integra en el paisaje, a la vez que se asoma a la enorme metrópolis. Todos los límites entre el interior y exterior desaparecen cuando los alzados frontal, lateral y posterior se abren para conectar los espacios internos con los jardines y las terrazas de los niveles. Dispone de cuarenta y cuatro paneles de cristal deslizantes que pueden esconderse cuando la ocasión lo requiera.

Questa casa, arroccata su una sottile striscia di terra sulle famose colline di Hollywood, è ben integrata nel paesaggio, sebbene si affacci alla metropoli. I limiti tra dentro e fuori scompaiono quando il lato frontale, quello laterale e quello posteriore si aprono per unire gli spazi interni con i giardini e le terrazze su vari livelli. La casa ha quarantaquattro pannelli scorrevoli di vetro che, se necessario, si possono celare.

Esta casa cravada num pequeno terreno das famosas colinas de Hollywood integra-se na paisagem e debruça-se simultaneamente sobre a enorme metrópole. Os limites interior e exterior desaparecem quando as paredes frontal, lateral e posterior se abrem para fundir os espaços internos da casa com os jardins e as varandas dos vários níveis, através de quarenta e quatro painéis de vidro que se ocultam sempre que necessário.

Det här huset, som ligger på en smal tomt i de välkända bergen i Hollywood, integreras med landskapet samtidigt som det sticker ut över den enorma metropolen. Alla gränser mellan interiören och exteriören försvinner när husets alla sidor öppnar sig för att koppla samman insidan med trädgårdarna och våningarnas terrasser. Det finns fyrtiofyra skjutpaneler i glas som kan döljas vid behov.

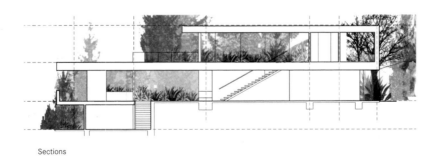

Sections

MIRÓ RIVERA ARCHITECTS
www.mirorivera.com
© Patrick Wong

The main purpose when this property in Austin, Texas (USA) was designed was to enhance the exterior via an open balcony to favor the impressive views that unfold all around. Both the lower and upper levels have glass balconies that afford generous views. The two levels become a beautiful showcase for the view and the living room. On the roof, of note is a pergola that separates this warm, pleasant place.

Le principal objectif, lors de la planification de cette maison située à Austin (Texas, États-Unis), a été de mettre l'extérieur en valeur avec un balcon ouvert, afin de profiter du panorama impressionnant qui s'étend tout autour. Aussi bien le niveau inférieur que le supérieur disposent de balcons vitrés offrant une vue généreuse. Les deux niveaux deviennent une belle vitrine qui permet d'apprécier la vue. Sur la terrasse, une pergola isolant ce lieu chaleureux et agréable se distingue.

Bei der Planung dieses Wohnhauses in Austin (Texas) stand die Einbeziehung der eindrucksvollen Aussicht auf die umgebende Landschaft im Vordergrund. Daher wurden in beiden Geschossen verglaste Balkone vorgesehen, die einen ungehinderten Ausblick ermöglichen. Entstanden ist so ein privilegierter Aufenthaltsbereich im Freien. Auf dem Flachdach schützt eine Pergola vor der Sonneneinstrahlung.

Hoofddoel bij het ontwerpen van dit huis in Austin (Texas, VS) was de buitenruimte te benadrukken door een open balkon met uitzicht op de indrukwekkende omgeving in te richten. Onder- en bovenverdieping beschikken beide over glazen balkons met een weids uitzicht. Beide verdiepingen zijn plekken geworden waar het goed toeven is. Op het dakterras zorgt een pergola voor de nodige beschutting.

El principal objetivo cuando se proyectó esta vivienda situada en Austin (Texas, Estados Unidos) fue potenciar el exterior mediante un balcón abierto para favorecer las impresionantes vistas. Por eso, tanto el nivel inferior como el superior disponen de balcones acristalados que los convierten en espacios ideales para relajarse y disfrutar de las vistas. En la azotea, destaca una pérgola que aísla este lugar cálido y agradable.

Nel progettare questa casa di Austin (Texas, Stati Uniti), l'obiettivo è stato creare un balcone aperto per favorire le splendide viste sul paesaggio circostante. Tanto il piano inferiore quanto quello superiore hanno balconi a vetri da cui si ammirano magnifici panorami. Entrambi i livelli si trasformano in una bella vetrina. Sul lastrico solare, spicca una pergola che isola questo luogo caldo e gradevole.

Quando se fez o projecto desta vivenda situada em Austin (Texas, Estados Unidos) o grande objectivo foi a potenciação do exterior através de uma varanda aberta para a vista deslumbrante que oferece. Essa é a razão pela qual as varandas, tanto o piso térreo como o primeiro andar, são envidraçadas. Na açoteia, destaca-se uma pérgula que protege do calor directo do sol e cria uma atmosfera agradável.

Huvudsyftet med det här projektet i Austin (Texas, USA), var att göra det yttre mer kraftfullt genom en öppen balkong för att framhäva den vackra utsikten. Både nedre och övre plan har inglasade balkonger som erbjuder fin utsikt. Båda våningarna blir till en vacker skådeplats för utsikten och vardagsrummet. På terrassen utmärker sig en pergola som avskärmar denna varma och trevliga plats.

This property in Yokohama, one of Tokyo's most densely populated suburbs, stands out for its L-shaped distribution. This angular structure permits the creation of multiple balconies with views onto the inner courtyard. The glassed-in façade and high porticos that form the terraces guarantee the entry of natural light.

Cette maison, située à Yokohama, l'une des banlieues les plus peuplées de Tokyo, se distingue par son agencement en forme de L. Cette structure angulaire permet la création de multiples balcons avec vue sur la cour intérieure. La façade vitrée et les hauts portiques qui forment la terrasse assurent le passage de la lumière du jour.

Dieses Einfamilienhaus in Yokohama, einem dicht besiedelten Vorort von Tokio, zeichnet sich durch seinen L-förmigen Grundriss aus. Die abgewinkelte Form erlaubt die Schaffung mehrerer Balkone mit Blick auf den Innenhof. Durch die großzügigen Glasflächen der Fassade und die hohen Vordächer über den Terrassen gelangt viel natürliches Licht in die Wohnräume.

Deze woning staat in Yokohama, een van de dichtstbevolkte voorsteden van Tokyo, en valt op door haar L-vorm. Door de vele hoeken kunnen veel balkons worden geplaatst die op de binnenplaats uitkijken. De glazen gevel en de hoge galerijen die gevormd worden door de terrassen zorgen voor een goede inval van daglicht.

Esta vivienda, situada en Yokohama, uno de los suburbios de Tokio con mayor densidad de población, destaca por su distribución en forma de L. Esta estructura angular permite la creación de múltiples balcones con vistas al patio interior. La fachada acristalada y los altos pórticos que forman las terrazas garantizan la entrada de luz natural.

Questa abitazione, sita a Yokohama, uno dei quartieri di Tokio caratterizzati da maggior densità di popolazione, fa spicco per la sua distribuzione a forma di L. Grazie a tale struttura angolare è stato possibile creare vari balconi con vista sul cortile interno. La facciata a vetri e gli elevati portici che formano le terrazze permettono il passaggio della luce naturale.

Esta vivenda, situada em Yokohama, um dos subúrbios de Tóquio mais densamente povoados da cidade, destaca-se pela sua distribuição em forma de L. Esta estrutura angular permite a criação de inúmeras varandas com vista para o pátio interior. A fachada envidraçada reflete a luz, garantindo a entrada da luz natural.

Den här bostaden i Yokohama, en av Tokyos folktätaste förorter, utmärker sig på grund av den L- formade planlösningen. Den här vinkelformade konstruktionen gör det möjligt att bygga flera balkonger med utsikt över innergården. Glasfasaden och de höga portikerna som utgör terrasserna släpper in ljus till ingången.

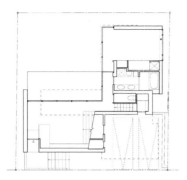

Ground floor

First floor

Elevations

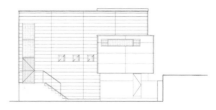

HOUSE IN **ORANJEZICHT**

VAN DER MERWE MISZEWSKI ARCHITECTS
www.vdmma.com
© Van der Merwe Miszewski Architects

This project was built on a 45-degree slope in a residential neighborhood of Cape Town. The house is surrounded by a dense pine forest and so the idea was to prioritize the views onto the inside. This goal was achieved by building multiple façade openings, using windows and balconies that guarantee the views over the surrounding landscape.

Ce projet s'élève sur une pente à 45°, dans une zone résidentielle du Cap. La maison est entourée d'une forêt de pins très dense. Pour cette raison, les vues de l'intérieur ont été privilégiées. L'objectif a été atteint grâce à la construction de multiples ouvertures dans la façade, au moyen de fenêtres et de balcons offrant une vue du paysage environnant.

In einem Wohnviertel von Kapstadt, auf einem Grundstück mit bis zu 45° Gefälle, liegt dieses Haus. Es ist von einem dichten Kiefernwald umgeben, weshalb man bei der Planung die Ausblicke in den Garten besonders berücksichtigt hat. Daher wurden viele großflächige Fenster und umlaufende Balkone vorgesehen, von denen aus man den Blick hinaus in die Natur genießen kann.

Dit gebouw staat op een helling van 45 graden, in een woonwijk van Kaapstad. De woning wordt omringd door een dicht naaldbomenbos. Om deze reden gaf men voorrang aan het uitzicht op het interieur. Dit doel werd bereikt door de vele openingen in de gevel: ramen en balkons, vanwaaruit men tevens uitzicht heeft op het omringende landschap.

Este proyecto se eleva sobre una pendiente de 45 grados, en una zona residencial de Ciudad del Cabo. La vivienda está rodeada por un denso bosque de pinos, por lo que se quisieron primar las vistas al interior. El objetivo se consiguió con la construcción de múltiples aberturas en la fachada, mediante ventanas y balcones que garantizan las vistas al paisaje circundante.

Questo progetto si eleva su una pendenza di 45 gradi, in una zona residenziale di Città del Capo. La casa è circondata da un fitto bosco di pini, pertanto si è voluto dare maggiore importanza alle viste dall'interno. L'obiettivo è stato raggiunto mediante la realizzazione di molteplici aperture lungo la facciata, con finestre e balconi da cui si godono splendide viste sul paesaggio circostante.

Este projecto eleva-se sobre uma inclinação de 45 graus, numa zona residencial da Cidade do Cabo. O facto de a vivenda estar rodeada por um denso pinhal fez com que se privilegiasse a vista para o interior. Este objectivo foi alcançado com a construção de várias aberturas na fachada, tais como janelas e varandas, que, simultaneamente, garantem a visão da paisagem envolvente.

Det här projektet reser sig över en 45- gradig sluttning i ett bostadsområde i Kapstaden. Bostaden omges av en tätbevuxen tallskog, vilket gjorde att man ville förbättra utsikten över insidan. Man nådde målet genom att bygga flera öppningar i fasaden i form av fönster och balkonger som möjliggör utsikt över det omgivande landskapet.

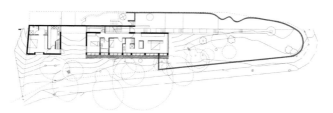

Ground floor

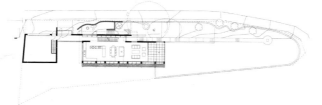

First floor

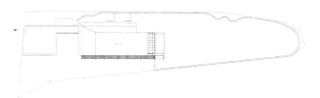

Second floor

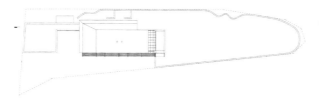

Roof plan

INSPIRATIONS: BALCONIES

BALCONS · BALKONS · BALKONS · BALCONES · BALCONI · VARANDAS · BALKONGER

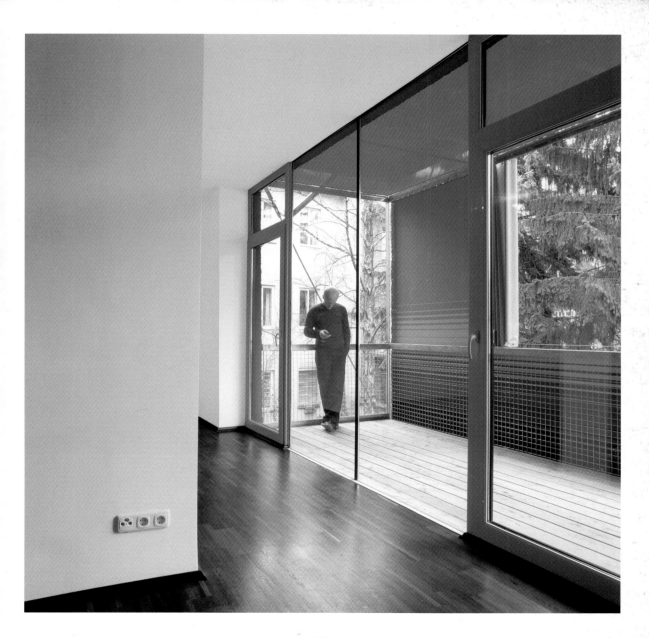

PATIOS

COURS · PATIOS · PATIO'S · PATIOS · CORTILI · PÁTIOS · PATIO

Patios, whether interior or exterior, can be considered the lungs of the home. The other rooms are distributed around them to make the most of the ventilation and natural light. Some have small gardens with a flowerbed or grass, flowers, or even trees with branches that often reach as high as the building. Sliding doors or fixed windows contribute to visual continuity while also protecting the interior. When there are a number of patios, each room, level or zone has its own outdoor exit.

Les cours, intérieures ou extérieures, peuvent être considérées comme le poumon de la maison. Les pièces restantes sont réparties autour de cet espace, afin de profiter au maximum de la ventilation et de la lumière du jour. Certaines cours proposent de petits jardins avec un parterre ou du gazon, des fleurs et même des arbres avec des branches pouvant atteindre la hauteur du bâtiment. Les portes coulissantes ou les fenêtres fixes favorisent la continuité visuelle, tout en protégeant l'intérieur. Lorsqu'il existe plusieurs cours, chaque pièce, niveau ou zone dispose de sa propre sortie vers l'extérieur.

Ein Innenhof ist wie die Lunge eines Hauses: Die Wohnräume sind um den Hof herum angeordnet und werden auf diese Weise optimal belüftet und mit natürlichem Licht versorgt. In manchen Innenhöfen gibt es kleine Gärten mit Blumenrabatten und Rasenflächen, zuweilen sogar Bäume, deren Zweige über das Dach des Gebäudes hinausreichen. Gläserne Schiebetüren oder großflächige Fenster erweitern den Innenraum visuell nach draußen, während sie vor ungünstigen Klimaeinflüssen schützen. Gibt es mehrere Innenhöfe, kann jeder Wohnraum bzw. jede Etage über einen eigenen Zugang zu den Außenbereichen verfügen.

Of patio's zich nu binnen of buiten bevinden, ze kunnen worden gezien als de long van een woning. De overige kamers bevinden zich rond deze ruimte om optimaal te kunnen profiteren van ventilatie en daglicht. Sommige patio's of binnenplaatsen zijn voorzien van borders, een klein gazon, bloemen of zelfs bomen die even hoog zijn als het gebouw waarin de patio zich bevindt. Schuifdeuren en ramen zorgen voor visuele continuïteit, terwijl ze tegelijkertijd de ruimte binnen afschermen. Als er meerdere patio's zijn, heeft elke kamer, verdieping of zone zijn eigen uitgang naar buiten.

Los patios, ya sean interiores o exteriores, pueden ser considerados como el pulmón de la vivienda. El resto de las habitaciones se distribuyen alrededor de este espacio para aprovechar al máximo la ventilación y la luz natural. Algunos cuentan con pequeños jardines con un parterre o césped, flores e incluso árboles que pueden alcanzar la altura del edificio. Las puertas correderas o las ventanas fijas favorecen la continuidad visual a la vez que protegen el interior. Cuando existen varios patios, cada habitación, nivel o zona dispone de su propia salida al exterior.

I cortili, che siano interni o esterni, possono essere considerati quali i polmoni della casa. Le altre stanze, di solito, si distribuiscono intorno a questo spazio per sfruttare al massimo la ventilazione e la luce naturale. Alcuni possiedono piccoli giardini con un parterre o un prato, fiori e perfino alberi con rami che possono eguagliare l'altezza dell'edificio. Le porte scorrevoli o le finestre fisse favoriscono la continuità visiva e, nel contempo, proteggono l'interno. Quando ci sono diversi cortili, ogni stanza, ogni piano o zona ha la sua uscita all'esterno.

Os pátios, quer sejam interiores quer exteriores, podem ser considerados como um pulmão da residência. O resto dos compartimentos circunda este espaço para tirar o máximo partido do arejamento e da luz natural. Alguns contam com pequenos jardins com canteiros ou relvados, flores e até árvores com copas que chegam a atingir a altura do edifício. Portas de correr ou janelas fixas favorecem a impressão de continuidade ao mesmo tempo que protegem a intimidade do interior. Na presença de vários pátios, cada compartimento, nível ou zona dispõe da sua própria saída para o exterior.

Patios, oavsett om de är interiöra eller exteriöra, kan anses vara bostadens lunga. Resten av rummen befinner sig runt detta utrymme för att utnyttja ventilationen och dagsljuset till fullo. Några rum har små trädgårdar med blomsterrabatter eller gräsmattor, blommor, och till och med träd med grenar som når ända upp till byggnadens högsta punkt. Skjutdörrarna och de fasta fönstren framhäver den visuella kontinuiteten samtidigt som de skyddar interiören. När det finns flera patios har varje rum, plan eller yta sin egen utgång till utomhusområdena.

EHRLICH ARCHITECTS
www.s-ehrlich.com
© Fernando Gómez/surpressagencia.com

This home in the heart of Venice, LA, was designed around one of the trees already on the plot. The architect and proprietor designed three patios: one out the front (the patio with the tree), another which is shared with the guesthouse; and a third close by the pool. The glassed-in areas open the home up to the outside while the textured elements merge the space with nature.

Cette maison, situé au cœur de Venice, à Los Angeles, a été planifiée autour d'arbres déjà présents sur le terrain. L'architecte et propriétaire a conçu trois cours : une devant (la cour de l'arbre), l'autre près de la maison des invités et une troisième cour à côté de la piscine. Les surfaces vitrées ouvrent la maison sur l'extérieur tandis que l'espace fusionne avec la nature grâce aux éléments texturés.

Das hier vorgestellte Haus steht in Venice, nahe Los Angeles. Es wurde so geplant, dass die Bäume auf dem Grundstück erhalten werden konnten. Architekt und Bauherr entwarfen drei Höfe: einen vorn (mit Baum), einen zweiten zwischen Haupthaus und Gästeappartement und den dritten beim Schwimmbecken. Über große Glasflächen öffnen sich die Wohnräume nach draußen und schaffen so eine Verbindung zur Natur.

Dit huis staat in het hart van Venice, Los Angeles. Het ontwerp sloot aan bij de bomen op het perceel. De architect – tevens eigenaar – ontwierp drie patio's: één aan de voorkant (met de boom), één bij het gastenverblijf en een derde dicht bij het zwembad. Door de glazen oppervlakken staat de woning in verbinding met het exterieur. De getextureerde elementen voegen ruimte en natuur samen.

Esta casa situada en el corazón de Venice, en Los Ángeles, fue proyectada alrededor de unos árboles que ya estaban en la parcela. El arquitecto y propietario diseñó tres patios: uno delantero (el patio del árbol), el otro compartido con la casa de invitados y un tercer patio próximo a la piscina. Las superficies acristaladas abren la vivienda al exterior mientras que los elementos texturizados fusionan el espacio con la naturaleza.

Questa casa sita nel cuore di Venice, a Los Angeles, è stata costruita intorno a alcuni alberi preesistenti. L'architetto, che è anche il proprietario, ha progettato tre cortili: uno davanti (il cortile dell'albero), uno in comune con la casa per gli ospiti e un terzo vicino alla piscina. Le superfici a vetri aprono l'abitazione all'esterno mentre gli elementi con texture fondono lo spazio con la natura.

Esta casa situada no centro de Veneza, em Los Angeles, foi projectada em redor de árvores existentes no terreno. O arquitecto e proprietário desenhou três pátios: um na frente (o pátio das árvores), outro junto dos aposentos dos convidados e o terceiro próximo da piscina. Superfícies envidraçadas abrem a vivenda ao exterior enquanto a textura dos elementos harmoniza o espaço com a natureza.

Det här huset i hjärtat av Venice, i Los Ángeles, utformades kring några träd som redan fanns på tomten. Arkitekten och ägaren ritade tre innergårdar: en på framsidan (innergården med träd), den andra som delas med gäststugan, och en tredje innergård intill poolen. De inglasade utrymmena gör att bostaden öppnas upp mot utsidan medan elementen med struktur sammanför utrymmet med naturen.

LOTUS HOUSE

KENGO KUMA & ASSOCIATES
www.kkaa.co.jp
© Daici Ano

The location of this plot next to a river suggested that the house should be surrounded by a lake. The resulting project is a volume with multiple openings, both for the shape of the patios and the configuration of the walls, where the voids and travertine sheets form a spectacular checkerboard. This meant the surrounding plant life and light could penetrate the property.

L'emplacement de ce terrain près d'une rivière a favorisé la création d'un bassin autour de cette maison. Le projet qui en a résulté est un volume avec de nombreuses ouvertures, aussi bien par la forme des cours que par la configuration des murs, où le vide et les plaques de travertin forment un spectaculaire damier. De cette manière, la végétation de l'environnement et la lumière entrent dans la maison.

Die Lage dieses Grundstücks an einem Flusslauf machte die Anlage eines kleinen Teiches um das Haus herum möglich. Entstanden ist ein Baukörper mit vielfältigen Öffnungen: Patios zwischen den Räumen und Fenster in den Außenwänden mit ihrem Schachbrettmuster aus Travertinplatten. So gelangt das Tageslicht bis in das Haus und das Grün der Vegetation dringt bis in die Innenräume vor.

Door de ligging van dit perceel bij een rivier kon rondom het huis een vijver worden aangelegd. Het resultaat is een ontwerp met meerdere openingen, zowel door de vorm van de patio's als door de vormgeving van de wanden, waar de open stukken en de platen van travertijn een spectaculair dambord vormen. Hierdoor komen het licht en het groen van de omgeving de woning binnen.

La ubicación de esta parcela junto a un río dio al arquitecto la idea de rodear la casa de un estanque. El proyecto resultante es un volumen con múltiples aberturas, tanto por la forma de los patios como por la configuración de las paredes, en las que el vacío y las placas de travertino forman un espectacular damero. De esta manera, la vegetación del entorno y la luz se adentran en la vivienda.

Grazie alla sua posizione, accanto a un fiume, è stato possibile circondare la casa con un laghetto. Il risultato è un volume con varie aperture, tanto per la forma dei cortili quanto per la configurazione delle pareti, nelle quali il vuoto e le lastre di travertino formano una magnifica scacchiera. In tal modo, la vegetazione circostante e la luce entrano nell'abitazione.

A localização deste terreno junto ao rio propiciou a construção de um lago a rodear a casa. O projecto resultante é um volume com múltiplas aberturas, tanto pela forma dos pátios como pela configuração das paredes, nas quais o vazio e as placas de travertino formam um espectacular tabuleiro de damas. Aquela disposição faz com que a vegetação em redor e a luz entrem pela vivenda.

Att denna fastighet låg bredvid en flod gav upphov till dammen som omger huset. Projektet resulterade i en enhet med flera öppningar, både genom innergårdarna och utformandet av väggarna, där öppningar och plattor av travertin skapar ett iögonfallande damspelsbräde. På det här sättet når den omgivande vegetationen och ljuset in i bostaden.

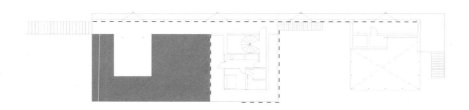

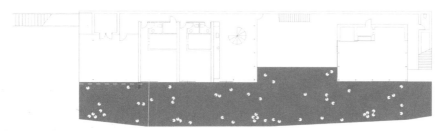

Plans

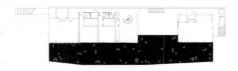

Plans

Elevations

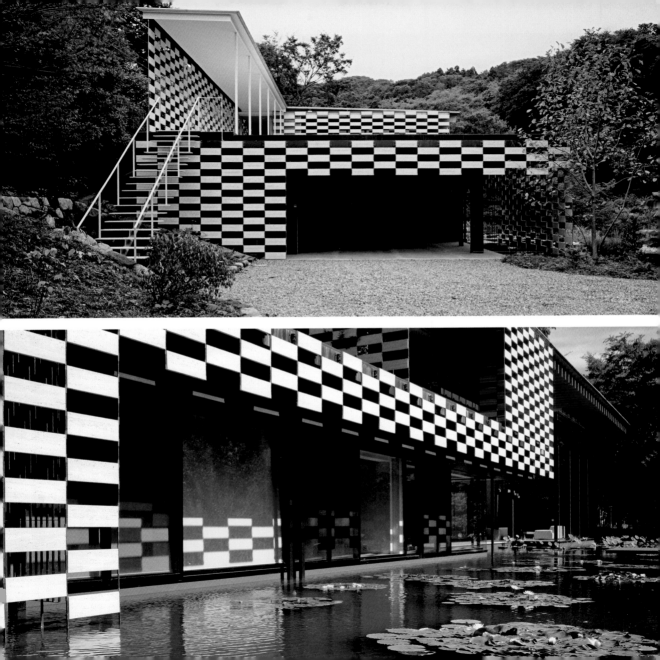

MARCIO KOGAN
www.marciokogan.com.br
© Arnaldo Pappalardo

Sited in an area of leafy vegetation, this house unfurls over a single L-shaped floor plan set around an extensive gardened courtyard. Both the façade walls and a large part of the interior ones are covered in pale, warm stone slabs. Running the length of the property, the stone sheets form an attractive frame for the courtyard, as if it were a painting.

Cette maison, située dans une zone de végétation luxuriante, se compose d'un seul niveau en forme de L autour d'une vaste cour aménagée en jardin. Aussi bien les murs de la façade qu'une grande partie des intérieurs sont recouverts de dalles de pierre calcaire claire. Sur le long de l'immeuble, ces plaques en pierre forment une jolie trame qui borde la cour à la manière d'un cadre.

In einer dicht bewaldeten Gegend liegt dieses eingeschossige Haus in L-Form mit seinem großen begrünten Patio. Sowohl die Mauer der Fassade als auch ein großer Teil der Wände im Inneren sind mit hellem Kalkstein verkleidet. Die abwechslungsreiche Oberfläche dieser Steinplatten beherrscht die Gesamtansicht des Gebäudes und bildet den Hintergrund, eine Art Rahmen, für den Gartenhof.

Dit huis van één woonlaag staat in een lommerijk gebied en is rond een ruime, groene patio gebouwd in een L-vorm. Zowel de gevel als een groot deel van de binnenvertrekken zijn bekleed met lichte kalkstenen tegels. Over de lengte van het hele pand vormen deze stenen een aantrekkelijke structuur die de patio als een schilderij omlijst.

Situada en una zona de vegetación frondosa, esta casa se desarrolla en una sola planta con forma de L en torno a un amplio patio ajardinado. Tanto los muros de la fachada como gran parte de los interiores están revestidos con losas de piedra caliza clara. A lo largo de todo el inmueble, estas planchas de piedra forman un atractivo entramado que enmarca el patio como si se tratara de un cuadro.

Sita in una zona dalla vegetazione lussureggiante, questa casa si sviluppa su un solo piano a forma di L intorno a un ampio cortile con giardino. Sia i muri della facciata sia gran parte degli interni sono rivestiti di mattonelle di pietra calcarea dai toni chiari. In tutto l'edificio, queste lastre di pietra formano una piacevole struttura che incornicia il cortile come se fosse un quadro.

Situada numa zona de vegetação frondosa, esta casa desenvolve-se num só piso em forma de L envolvendo um amplo pátio ajardinado. Tanto as paredes da fachada como grande parte dos interiores estão revestidos com lousas de pedra calcária clara. Ao longo de todo o imóvel, estas lâminas de pedra formam uma trama atractiva que emoldura o pátio convertendo-o numa espécie de quadro.

Den här bostaden befinner sig på en enda L-formad våning runt en rymlig innergård med trädgård. Både fasaden och stora delar av innerväggarna har beklätts med plattor av ljus kalksten. Längs hela byggnaden bildar dessa stenplattor ett vackert nät som ramar in innergården likt en tavla.

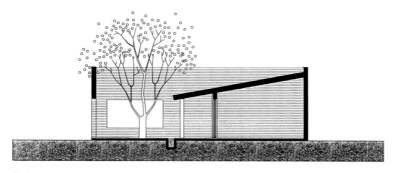

Section

ESTUDIO RINALDI & ASOCIADOS
www.estudiorinaldi.com
© Wade Zimmerman

The remodeling of this duplex, located in a classic brownstone on New York's Upper West Side, consisted principally in doing up the passageway and attaining a light effect from the rear patio. Features of the new terrace layout are the elegant Brazilian quartzite walls and warm French stone, perfectly offset by the darker, warm granite flooring and red cedar benches.

Le réaménagement de ce duplex, situé dans une *brownstone* classique de l'Upper West Side newyorkais, consistait principalement à utiliser le passage et l'effet de la lumière depuis la cour arrière. La nouvelle disposition de cette terrasse met en valeur les élégants murs en quartzite brésilien et la pierre calcaire d'origine française, qui s'harmonisent parfaitement avec le sol en pierre calcaire plus sombre et granitique ainsi qu'avec les bancs en cèdre rouge.

Beim Umbau dieser Maisonette-Wohnung in einem typischen Backsteingebäude der New Yorker Upper West Side wurde großer Wert auf die Nutzung des Tageslichts gelegt, das über den Hinterhof eindringt. Besonders überzeugend ist die Kombination eleganter Wände aus brasilianischem Quarz und französischem Kalkstein mit dunklerem Kalkstein und Granit als Bodenbelag und den Bänken aus rotem Zedernholz.

De renovatie van deze duplexwoning in een klassieke *brownstone* in Upper West Side in New York moest met name zorgen voor een goede lichtinval vanuit de patio aan de achterkant. In de nieuwe indeling van het terras vallen de elegante wanden van Braziliaans kwartsiet en het Franse kalksteen op, die volmaakt passen bij de wat donkerder kalkstenen en granieten vloer en bij de banken van rood cederhout.

La remodelación de este dúplex, situado en un clásico *brownstone* del Upper West Side neoyorquino, se centró en adecuar la entrada de la luz desde el patio trasero. En la nueva disposición de esta terraza destacan las elegantes paredes de cuarcita brasileña y la piedra caliza de origen francés, que casan a la perfección con el suelo de caliza más oscura y granítica y con los bancos de cedro rojo.

La ristrutturazione di questo duplex, sito in un classico *brownstone* dell'Upper West Side newyorchese, è consistita principalmente nel migliorare il passaggio e l'effetto della luce proveniente dal cortile posteriore. Sulla terrazza spiccano le eleganti pareti di quarzite brasiliana e la pietra calcarea francese, che si combinano alla perfezione con il pavimento di pietra calcarea più scura e granitica nonché con le panchine di cedro rosso.

A remodelação deste duplex, situado num clássico *brownstone* do Upper West Side nova-iorquino, ambicionava sobretudo adequar a passagem e o efeito da luz vinda do pátio traseiro. Na nova disposição deste terraço, destacam-se as elegantes paredes de quartzo brasileiro e a pedra calcária de origem francesa, em combinação perfeita com o chão de granito e calcário mais escuro e com os bancos em cedro vermelho.

Ombyggnaden av den här etagevåningen, i en klassisk brownstone- byggnad i New Yorks Upper West Side, bestod huvudsakligen i att anpassa passagen och ljuseffekten från den bakre pation. På den här nya terrassen utmärker sig de eleganta väggarna av brasiliansk kvarts och kalkstenen av franskt ursprung, som passar perfekt ihop med stengolvet av mörkare kalk och granit samt bänkarna i rött cederträ.

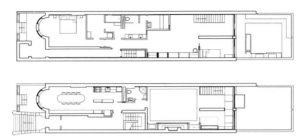

Plan

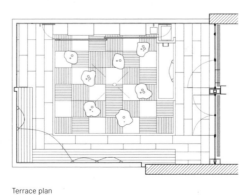

Terrace plan

M3 ARCHITECTS
www.m3architects.com
© M3 Architects

The project for this Victorian-style house, located in the middle of the Highbury Fields conservation area in the London neighborhood of Islington, consisted of expanding a single floor by glassing-in the rear of the property. The proposed structural focus creates physical and visual freedom and generates a new spatial relationship with the courtyard.

Le projet de cette maison de style victorien, située au centre de la zone protégée de Highbury Fields, dans le quartier londonien d'Islington, consiste en l'agrandissement d'un seul étage par la création d'une baie vitrée sur la partie arrière de la demeure. L'approche structurelle proposée crée une liberté physique et visuelle et génère une nouvelle relation de l'espace avec la cour.

Im Zuge des Umbaus dieses viktorianischen Anwesens im denkmalgeschützten Bereich Highbury Fields im Londoner Stadtviertel Islington wurde der hintere Teil der im Erdgeschoss liegenden Wohnung verglast. Auf diese Weise konnte der Wohnraum optisch und physisch erheblich erweitert und eine völlig neue Wechselbeziehung zum Gartenhof geschaffen werden.

Het ontwerp voor dit huis in victoriaanse stijl in het centrum van het beschermde stadsgebied van Highbury Fields in de Londense wijk Islington bestond uit de uitbreiding van één verdieping door de achterzijde van de woning van glas te maken. De gewijzigde structuur creëert visuele en fysieke vrijheid en zorgt voor een nieuwe ruimtelijke verbinding met de patio.

El proyecto de esta casa de estilo victoriano, situada en el centro de la zona de conservación de Highbury Fields, en el barrio londinense de Islington, consiste en la ampliación de una sola planta mediante el acristalamiento de la parte trasera de la vivienda. El enfoque estructural propuesto crea libertad física y visual y genera una nueva relación espacial con el patio.

Il progetto di questa casa in stile vittoriano, nel mezzo della zona di conservazione di Highbury Fields, nel quartiere londinese di Islington, consiste nell'ampliamento di un solo piano mediante l'invetriatura della parte posteriore dell'abitazione. L'approccio strutturale proposto apporta libertà fisica e visiva instaurando, nel contempo, un nuovo rapporto spaziale con il cortile.

O projecto desta casa de estilo vitoriano, situada no centro da zona de conservação de Highbury Fields, no bairro londrino de Islington, consiste na ampliação de um piso único, e para tal a parte traseira da vivenda foi envidraçada. O enfoque estrutural proposto cria maior liberdade física e visual e contribui para gerar uma nova relação espacial com o pátio.

Renoveringen av det här huset i viktoriansk stil, i centrum av det bevarade området Highbury Fields i Londonstadsdelen Islington, bestod i utvidgandet av en enda våning genom att inglasa den bakre delen av bostaden. Detta byggnadsmässiga fokus framkallar fysisk och visuell frihet samt skapar ett nytt rumsligt förhållande till pation.

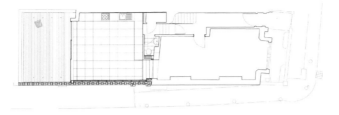

Ground floor

Side elevation

ANNIE RESIDENCE

BERCY CHEN STUDIO
www.bcarc.com
© Mike Osborne

This house was built for two families, so it has two habitable areas, i.e., volumes connected by a glass corridor. Each building has a central nucleus of a steel structure covered in red or blue acrylic panels that contains the service zones. The pool is the focal point of the project, around which all the other rooms in the house are distributed.

Cette maison a été construite pour deux familles et c'est pourquoi elle dispose de deux zones habitables : deux volumes reliés par un couloir vitré. Chaque bâtiment possède un noyau central doté d'une structure en acier couverte de panneaux acryliques de couleur rouge ou bleue qui renferme les différentes pièces. La piscine est le point central du projet autour duquel s'organisent toutes les pièces de la maison.

Da es sich bei diesem Gebäude um ein Zweifamilienhaus handelt, ist es in zwei Wohnbereiche unterteilt, deren Baukörper über einen verglasten Gang miteinander verbunden sind. Der zentrale Kern jedes der beiden Blöcke besteht aus einer mit roten und blauen Acrylpanelen verkleideten Stahlstruktur, in der die Sanitäranlagen untergebracht sind. Das Schwimmbecken bildet den Mittelpunkt der Raumplanung.

Dit huis werd gebouwd voor twee gezinnen en heeft daarom twee woongedeelten, die via een glazen gang met elkaar verbonden zijn. Elk gebouw heeft een centrale kern bestaande uit een stalen structuur bekleed met panelen van rood en blauw acryl waarin de nodige installaties zijn ondergebracht. Het zwembad is het centrale punt van het ontwerp. Daaromheen liggen alle vertrekken van het huis.

Esta casa fue construida para dos familias, por eso cuenta con dos zonas habitables: dos volúmenes conectados por un pasillo acristalado. Cada edificio posee un núcleo central que consta de una estructura de acero recubierta de paneles acrílicos de color rojo o azul que contienen las zonas de servicios. La piscina es el punto central del proyecto, y a su alrededor se distribuyen todas las estancias de la casa.

Progettata per due famiglie, questa casa ha due zone abitative: due volumi collegati da un corridoio a vetri. Ogni edificio possiede un nucleo centrale formato da una struttura d'acciaio ricoperta di pannelli acrilici di colore rosso o blu che contengono le zone di servizi. La piscina è il punto centrale del progetto intorno al quale si distribuiscono tutte le stanze della casa.

Esta casa foi construída para duas famílias. Para esse fim, inclui duas zonas habitáveis: dois volumes ligados por um corredor envidraçado. Cada edifício possui um núcleo central que consta de uma estrutura de aço coberta de painéis acrílicos de cor vermelha ou azul contendo as zonas de serviço A piscina é o ponto central do projecto em redor da qual se distribuem todas as componentes da casa.

Det här huset byggdes till två familjer, därför har det två bostadsytor: två delar som kopplats samman genom en inglasad gång. Varje byggnad har en central kärna, bestående av en aluminiumkonstruktion som beklätts med akrylpaneler i rött eller blått, där man finner badrummen. Poolen är projektets centrala inslag, runt vilket alla husets rum befinner sig.

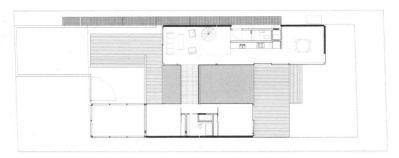

Ground floor

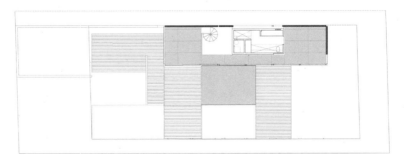

First floor

EDWARD SUZUKI ASSOCIATES
www.edward.net
© Nacasa & Partners

This three-storey home in Tokyo, with a large terrace on the top floor, has a recurring element in the three levels, i.e., terraces and patios, which permit the interior to be connected with the outside. These spaces mean many of the rooms enjoy natural lighting all day long, as well as good ventilation. The house has a tatami, where the inhabitants can take their meals in the traditional fashion.

Cette maison de trois étages à Tokyo, avec une grande terrasse à l'étage supérieur, possède un élément récurrent sur les trois niveaux : des terrasses et des cours, de sorte que l'intérieur est relié à l'extérieur. Ces baies vitrées permettent à de nombreuses chambres de bénéficier de la lumière naturelle tout au long de la journée, en plus de la ventilation adaptée. La maison dispose d'un tatami sur lequel les habitants peuvent manger selon la manière traditionnelle.

Dieses dreigeschossige Haus in Tokio zeichnet sich durch eine Vielzahl von Terrassen und Höfen aus, die das Innere mit dem Äußeren verbinden. Die größte Terrasse liegt im obersten Stockwerk. Die Aussparungen sorgen dafür, dass die Innenräume ausreichend mit Frischluft versorgt werden und so viel Tageslicht wie möglich erhalten. Es gibt auch einen Tatami, um traditionelles japanisches Essen zu genießen.

Dit huis van drie verdiepingen in Tokyo met een groot terras op de bovenverdieping beschikt over elementen die op alle verdiepingen terugkomen: terrassen en patio's. Hierdoor is binnen verbonden met buiten. Doordat de ruimten open zijn, beschikken veel vertrekken de hele dag over daglicht en een goede ventilatie. Op de tatami kunnen de bewoners op traditionele wijze van de maaltijd genieten.

Esta casa de tres pisos de Tokio, con una gran terraza en la planta superior, posee un elemento recurrente en los tres niveles: terrazas y patios, lo que permite que el interior esté conectado con el exterior. Estos vanos hacen que muchas habitaciones dispongan de luz natural a lo largo del día, además de la ventilación adecuada. La casa tiene un tatami en el que los habitantes pueden disfrutar de las comidas al estilo tradicional.

Questa casa di Tokyo disposta su tre piani, con una grande terrazza al livello superiore, presenta un elemento ricorrente: terrazze e cortili, che collegano l'interno con l'esterno. Grazie a queste aree, molte stanze hanno luce naturale di giorno, oltre a un'adeguata ventilazione. La casa possiede un *tatami* su cui è possibile mangiare alla maniera tradizionale.

Esta casa de três pisos, em Tóquio, com um grande terraço no piso superior, oferece terraços e pátios, em cada piso, o que permite que o interior esteja em comunicação direta com o exterior. Estes vãos fazem com que muitos compartimentos usufruam de luz natural ao longo do dia, além de ventilação adequada. A casa tem um tatame onde os habitantes podem saborear a comida ao estilo tradicional.

Det här trevåningshuset i Tokyo, med en stor terrass på översta våningen, har ett återkommande inslag på de tre våningarna: terrasser och innergårdar, vilka kopplar samman insidan med utsidan. Dessa öppningar gör att många rum, förutom att de får lagom mycket ventilering, får dagsljus hela dagen. I huset finns en tatamimatta där de boende kan avnjuta mat på traditionellt vis.

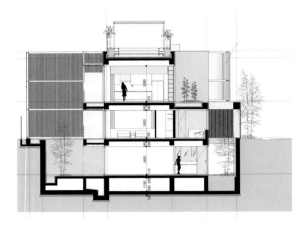

Cross section

First floor

HOLLIN & RADOSKE ARCHITEKTEN
www.hollinradoske.de
© Ludger Paffrath

This penthouse is found in a building from 1954. Following various renovations, the daytime area was distributed around two open courtyards that allow the natural light to enter. One is surrounded by a bamboo garden and features a hydromassage bathtub and shower. The other, covered in wood, was turned into a mediation area and has clear Eastern inspirations.

Cet appartement en attique est situé dans un ancien bâtiment de 1954. Après plusieurs rénovations, la zone de séjour a été distribuée autour des deux cours ouvertes qui laissent passer la lumière du jour. Une des cours est entourée d'un jardin en bambou et dispose d'une baignoire avec hydromassage et douche. L'autre cour, recouverte de bois, a été aménagée en zone de méditation et s'inspire manifestement de l'Orient.

Dieses Penthouse liegt in einem Gebäude aus dem Jahre 1954. Nach mehreren Umgestaltungen wurde der Wohnbereich um zwei Innenhöfe angeordnet, über die das Tageslicht in die Räume einfällt. In einem der Patios wurde ein Bambusgarten mit Whirlpool und Dusche angelegt. Der andere Patio zeigt eindeutig ostasiatische Anklänge und dient mit seinem Holzfußboden als Meditationsbereich.

Deze bovenverdieping bevindt zich in een oud gebouw uit 1954. Na enkele renovaties werd de zone voor overdag ingedeeld rond de twee open patio's, die daglicht binnenlaten. Een van de patio's heeft rondom een met bamboe beplante tuin met een hydromassagebad en een douche. De andere, met hout beklede patio is geschikt voor meditatie en is duidelijk oosters geïnspireerd.

Este ático se sitúa en un antiguo edificio de 1954. Después de varias renovaciones, la zona de día se distribuyó alrededor de dos patios abiertos que dejan pasar la luz natural. Uno de los patios está rodeado por un jardín de bambú y dispone de bañera de hidromasaje y ducha. El otro patio, recubierto de madera, se habilitó como zona de meditación y está claramente inspirada en Oriente.

Questo attico si trova in un edificio del 1954. Dopo varie ristrutturazioni, la zona giorno è stata distribuita intorno a due cortili aperti che fanno passare la luce naturale. Uno dei cortili è circondato da un giardino di bambù e possiede vasca con idromassaggio e doccia. L'altro cortile, rivestito di legno, è stato adibito a zona di meditazione in uno stile chiaramente orientale.

Este apartamento situa-se no último andar de um antigo edifício de 1954. Após várias renovações, a zona mais utilizada durante o dia distribuiu-se à volta dos pátios abertos que deixam passar a luz natural. Um dos pátios está rodeado por um jardim de bambu e dispõe de banheira de hidromassagem e duche. Outro pátio foi destinado a zona de meditação de clara inspiração oriental.

Den här vindsvåningen ligger i en gammal byggnad från 1954. Efter flera renoveringar placerades vardagsrummet runt två öppna innergårdar som låter dagsljuset komma in. En av innergårdarna omges av en bambuträdgård och har badkar med vattenmassage och dusch. Den andra innergården, som beklätts med trä, iordningställdes som meditationsutrymme och har klara inspirationskällor från Orienten.

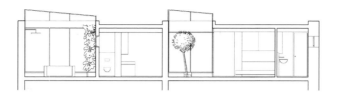

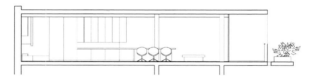

Sections

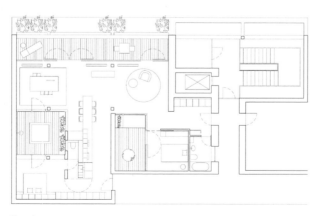

Floor plan

HOUSE **IN TAKANOHARA**

KENJI TAGASHIRA
www.kenji-tagashira.com
© Kei Sugino

This house in a small town in the district of Nara, Japan, seeks harmony between the interior and exterior spaces. The house opens outward via a large central courtyard that most of the rooms give onto. Enormous sliding windows permit access to a small garden at the same level as the living and dining rooms and also guarantee their ventilation.

Cette maison située dans une petite agglomération de la ville de Nara, au Japon, cherche l'harmonie entre les espaces intérieurs et extérieurs. La maison s'ouvre vers l'extérieur par une grande cour centrale, sur laquelle donnent la plupart des pièces. De très grandes baies vitrées coulissantes permettent d'accéder à un petit jardin situé au même niveau que le salon et la salle à manger, tout en assurant la ventilation de ces pièces.

Das hier gezeigte Haus liegt in einem Dorf im japanischen Nara-Distrikt und ist ein Beispiel für das Streben nach Harmonie zwischen Drinnen und Draußen. Über einen zentralen Innenhof, der die meisten Wohnräume mit Licht und Luft versorgt, öffnet sich das Haus nach draußen. Große Schiebefenster erlauben den Zugang zu einem kleinen Garten, der sich auf der gleichen Ebene befindet wie Wohn- und Esszimmer.

Dit huis staat in een dorpje in het Nara-district in Japan. Er is gezocht naar harmonie tussen de ruimten binnen en buiten. Het huis staat in verbinding met de buitenwereld via een grote, centrale patio waarop de meeste vertrekken uitkijken. Via enkele grote schuiframen komt men in een tuintje dat zich op hetzelfde niveau bevindt als de salon en eetkamer. De ramen zorgen voor een goede ventilatie.

Esta casa situada en una pequeña población del distrito de Nara, en Japón, busca la armonía entre los espacios interiores y exteriores. La casa se abre hacia el exterior mediante un gran patio central al que dan la mayoría de las estancias. Unas enormes ventanas correderas permiten el acceso a un pequeño jardín situado al mismo nivel que el salón y el comedor, además de garantizar la ventilación de estas habitaciones.

Costruita in un paesino del distretto di Nara, in Giappone, questa residenza ricerca l'armonia tra lo spazio interno e l'esterno. Si apre all'esterno grazie a un grande cortile centrale su cui si affaccia la maggior parte delle stanze. Attraverso enormi finestre scorrevoli, si ha accesso a un piccolo giardino che garantisce l'aerazione del soggiorno e della sala da pranzo.

Esta casa situada numa pequena povoação no distrito de Nara, no Japão, busca a harmonia entre os espaços interiores e exteriores. A casa abre-se para o exterior mediante um grande pátio central para o qual dão a maioria dos aposentos. Umas enormes vidraças de correr permitem o acesso a um pequeno jardim, situado ao mesmo nível da sala de estar e da sala de jantar, além de garantirem a circulação do ar.

Det här huset i ett litet samhälle i distriktet Nara, i Japan, eftersöker harmoni mellan insidan och utsidan. Huset öppnar upp sig mot området utanför genom en stor patio i mitten, mot vilken de flesta rummen vetter. Några enorma skjutfönster gör det möjligt att nå en liten trädgård på samma plan som vardagsrummet och matsalen, förutom att de förser de här rummen med ventilation.

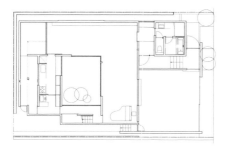

Ground floor

First floor

North elevation

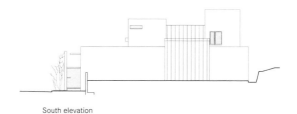

South elevation

Section

Section

This garden house is inspired by previous architectural projects, such as Featherston House designed by Robin Boyd in 1967. Small hanging gardens positioned on platforms at different levels climb down to other interior gardens and even a waterfall. The stairs group the different levels into which the interior spaces, such as the dining room, kitchen and living room, are distributed.

Cette maison jardin s'inspire de projets architecturaux précédents, comme la maison Featherston conçue par Robin Boyd en 1967. De petits jardins suspendus placés sur des plates-formes à différents niveaux donnent sur d'autres jardins intérieurs et même sur une cascade. Un escalier regroupe les différents niveaux où sont répartis les espaces intérieurs, comme la salle à manger, la cuisine ou le salon.

Der Entwurf dieses Hauses lehnt sich an andere Bauprojekte an, wie etwa das Haus Featherstone von Robin Boyd (1967). Plattformen auf verschiedenen Ebenen bieten Platz für kleine hängende Gärten, die in weitere, innen liegende Gärten übergehen und sogar einen Wasserfall bieten. Über Treppen sind die unterschiedlichen Ebenen der Innenräume miteinander verbunden: Esszimmer, Küche und Wohnzimmer.

Dit huis is geïnspireerd op eerder gemaakte ontwerpen, zoals dat voor het Featherston House van Robin Boyd uit 1967. De kleine hangende tuinen die op platforms op verschillende niveaus zijn aangelegd, lopen over in andere tuinen binnen, en zelfs in een waterval. De trappen voegen de verschillende niveaus samen, waar vertrekken zoals de eetkamer, keuken en salon zich bevinden.

Esta casa jardín está inspirada en proyectos arquitectónicos anteriores, como la casa Featherston diseñada por Robin Boyd en 1967. Pequeños jardines colgantes colocados sobre plataformas a distintos niveles se descuelgan a otros jardines interiores e incluso a una cascada. Las escaleras agrupan los distintos niveles en los que se distribuyen los espacios interiores, como el comedor, la cocina o el salón.

Questa casa-giardino è ispirata a progetti architettonici precedenti, come la residenza Featherston realizzata da Robin Boyd nel 1967. Piccoli giardini pensili su piattaforme a vari livelli «cadono» su altri giardini interni e perfino su una cascata. Le scale organizzano i vari livelli in cui si trovano gli spazi interni, come la sala da pranzo, la cucina o il soggiorno.

Esta casa jardim inspirou-se em projectos arquitectónicos anteriores, como a casa Featherston desenhada por Robin Boyd em 1967. Pequenos jardins suspensos sobre plataformas a níveis diversos pendem para outros jardins interiores e incluso para uma cascata. Por escadas se acede aos diversos níveis, sobre os quais se distribuem os espaços interiores, como zona de refeições, cozinha e salão.

Det här huset med trädgård har fått inspiration från tidigare arkitektoniska projekt, som Featherstonhuset, som ritades av Robin Boyd 1967. Små hängande trädgårdar, på olika plan, beblandar sig med andra trädgårdar och till och med ett vattenfall. Trapporna förenar de olika våningsplanen, där inomhusytorna- till exempel matsalen, köket och vardagsrummet- befinner sig.

CALLAS SHORTRIDGE
www.callas-shortridge.com
© Undine Pröhl

This patio with a jacuzzi is the ideal place to relax after a hard day's work. The jacuzzi is set apart from the other outdoor living areas and has a seat in which to relax. The combination of natural colors and materials creates a harmonious ambiance – the different shades of green, brown and red form a perfect match with the foliage the surrounds the space.

Cette cour avec un jacuzzi est le lieu idéal pour se reposer après une dure journée de travail. Le jacuzzi est isolé des autres espaces extérieurs et doté d'un siège pour se relaxer. Le mélange des couleurs et des matériaux naturels crée une ambiance harmonieuse : les différents tons de vert, marron et rouge forment un ensemble parfait avec le feuillage qui entoure l'espace.

Ein Whirlpool im Hof – der ideale Ort, um sich nach einem anstrengenden Arbeitstag zu entspannen. Der Pool ist von den anderen Außenbereichen abgeschirmt und verfügt über einen Ruhesitz. Die Kombination natürlicher Materialien und Farben schafft ein harmonisches Ambiente: Die verschiedenen Grün- Braun- und Rottöne nehmen die Farben des Blattwerks auf, das diesen Ort überschattet.

Deze patio met jacuzzi is een ideale plek om te relaxen na een zware werkdag. De jacuzzi is afgescheiden van de andere buitenvertrekken en heeft een zitje om te kunnen ontspannen. De combinatie van natuurlijke kleuren en materialen schept een harmonieuze sfeer: verschillende tinten groen, bruin en rood vormen een volmaakte eenheid met het omringende groen.

Este patio con *jacuzzi* es un lugar ideal para descansar después de un duro día de trabajo. El *jacuzzi* está aislado de las otras áreas de estar exteriores y dispone de un asiento para relajarse. La combinación de colores y materiales naturales crea un ambiente armónico: los diferentes tonos de verde, marrón y rojo forman un conjunto perfecto con el follaje que envuelve el espacio.

Questo cortile con *jacuzzi* è un luogo ideale per riposare dopo una dura giornata di lavoro. La *jacuzzi* è isolata dalle altre zone esterne e possiede un sedile per rilassarsi. La combinazione di colori e materiali naturali crea un ambiente equilibrato: le varie sfumature di verde, marrone e rosso formano un insieme perfetto con le foglie circostanti.

Este pátio com *jacuzzi* é o lugar ideal para descansar depois de um duro dia de trabalho. O *jacuzzi* está isolado das outras áreas de estar exteriores e dispõe de um assento para se relaxar. A combinação de cores e materiais naturais cria um ambiente harmónico: diferentes tons de verde, castanho e vermelho formam um conjunto perfeito com a folhagem que envolve o espaço.

Den här innergården med jacuzzi är den ideala platsen för vilostunder efter en hård arbetsdag. Jacuzzin har avskilts från de andra uterummen och har en sittplats där man kan slappna av. Kombinationen av naturliga färger och material skapar en harmonisk miljö: de olika nyanserna av grönt, brunt och rött bildar en perfekt helhet med växterna som omsluter utrymmet.

HAKUU-KAN

YOJI SASAKI, AKIRA SAKAMOTO
www.akirasakamoto.com
© Kei Sugino

Hakuu-Kan is a residential complex whose white walls interlace to create different types of open spaces: a parking area, a garden of sand and a number of secondary patios. The project was designed on the basis of aspects such as light, color, wind and water. The vegetation is composed of bamboo, horsetail, Japanese maples and lilies of the valley.

Hakuu-Kan est un complexe résidentiel dont les murs blancs s'entrelacent pour créer des espaces ouverts de différentes typologies : zone de parking, jardin de sable et plusieurs cours secondaires. Le projet a été conçu à partir d'éléments comme la lumière, la couleur, le vent et l'eau. La végétation se compose de bambous, de prêles, d'érables japonais et de muguets.

Hakuu-Kan ist ein Wohnkomplex, dessen weiße Mauern ineinander verschlungen sind und offene Räume unterschiedlicher Nutzung schaffen: Stellplätze, Sandgärten und mehrere kleine Innenhöfe. Das Projekt orientiert sich vor allem an der Wechselwirkung von Licht, Farbe, Wind und Wasser. Die Bepflanzung besteht aus Bambus, Schachtelhalm, japanischem Ahorn und Maiglöckchen.

Hakuu-Kan is een wooncomplex waarvan de witte muren zodanig zijn vervlochten dat open ruimten met verschillende functies zijn gecreëerd: een parkeerzone, een tuin en nog een aantal kleinere patio's. Uitgangspunten van het ontwerp zijn lucht, kleur, wind en water. De vegetatie wordt gevormd door bamboe, paardenstaart, Japanse esdoorn en lelietjes-van-dalen.

Hakuu-Kan es un complejo residencial cuyos muros blancos se entrelazan para crear espacios abiertos de diferentes tipologías: zona de aparcamiento, jardín de arena y varios patios secundarios. El proyecto ha sido concebido partiendo de aspectos como la luz, el color, el viento y el agua. La vegetación está compuesta por bambú, cola de caballo, arces japoneses y lirios del valle.

Il Hakuu-Kan è un complesso residenziale con muri bianchi che s'intrecciano per formare spazi aperti di vari tipi: zona parcheggio, giardino di sabbia e diversi cortili secondari. Il progetto è stato concepito partendo da elementi quali la luce, il colore, il vento e l'acqua. La vegetazione è composta da bambù, equiseti, aceri giapponesi e mughetti.

Hakuu-Kan é um complexo residencial cujas paredes brancas se entrelaçam para criar espaços abertos de diferentes tipologias: parque de estacionamento, jardim de areia e vários pátios secundários. O projecto foi concebido a partir de pressupostos considerando a luz, a cor, o vento e a água. Espécies diversas, desde bambu, cauda de cavalo, aceres japoneses a lírios do campo, compõem a vegetação.

Hakuu- Kan är ett bostadskomplex vars vita murar flätas samman för att skapa öppna utrymmen av olika karaktär: parkeringsplats, sandträdgård och flera mindre innergårdar. Projektet har planerats utifrån från aspekter som ljus, färg, vind och vatten. Växtligheten består av bambu, hästsvans, japansk lönn och liljekonvalj.

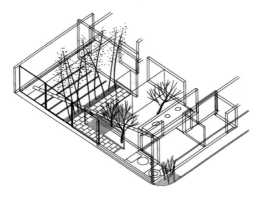

Perspective

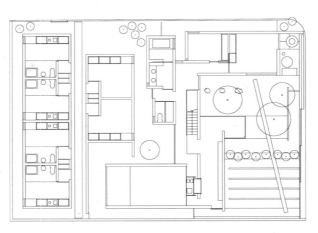

Plan

This patio is attached to the home's master suite and is characterized by a personal and exclusive style. The staircase has been extended with a long platform that stops before it reaches the ends to create a walkway among trees with music. From the end of this L-shaped platform of Ipe wood and through to the balcony wall, a number of pot plants with trees and plants are placed on large white stones.

Cette cour est une annexe de la suite matrimoniale de cette maison qui se caractérise par un style personnel et exclusif. Afin de créer une allée entre arbres et musique, le passage a été marqué avec une longue estrade qui n'atteint pas les extrémités. De la fin de cette plate-forme en L en bois d'ipé au mur du balcon, de grands pots avec des arbres et des plantes ont été placés sur des pierres blanches.

Dieser Patio liegt vor dem Schlafzimmer der Eigentümer und zeichnet sich durch einen sehr persönlichen Gestaltungsstil aus. Geschaffen wurde ein rhythmisch angelegter Spazierweg über einen langen Steg, der jedoch nicht von einer Wand bis zur anderen reicht. Am Ende dieser Terrasse in L-Form aus Ipe-Holz wurden bis zur Balkonmauer große Topfpflanzen und Kübel mit Bäumen auf die weißen Steine gestellt.

Deze patio ligt naast de ouderslaapkamer van de woning en bezit een persoonlijke, exclusieve stijl. Om een pad tussen bomen en muziek te creëren wordt de route aangegeven door een lange plankenvloer die niet helemaal doorloopt tot de uiteinden. Vanaf het verste punt van dit L-vormige plankier van ipéhout tot de muur van het balkon zijn op witte stenen grote bakken met bomen en planten geplaatst.

Este patio se encuentra anexo a la *suite* de matrimonio de esta vivienda y se caracteriza por un estilo personal y exclusivo. Para crear un paseo entre árboles y música, se han marcado los pasos mediante una tarima larga que no llega a los extremos. Desde el fin de esta plataforma en L de madera de ipé y hasta el muro del balcón, se han colocado sobre unas piedras blancas grandes macetas con árboles y plantas.

Questo cortile è annesso a una *suite* matrimoniale e si distingue per il suo stile personale nonché esclusivo. Per passeggiare tra gli alberi e la musica, è stato tracciato un lungo assito che non arriva fino alle estremità. Nel percorso compreso tra la fine di questa piattaforma a L di legno di ipè e il muro del balcone, sono stati posti grandi vasi con alberi e piante su pietre bianche.

Este pátio encontra-se anexo à *suite* de casal desta vivenda e caracteriza-se por um estilo pessoal e exclusivo. Para criar um caminho entre as árvores e a música, construiu-se um estrado sobre o comprido, em madeira de ipé, sem atingir os extremos. Desde as pontas desta plataforma em L, até à parede da varanda, colocaram-se, sobre pedras brancas, grandes vasos com árvores e plantas.

Den här innergården befinner sig intill denna bostads "svit" och kännetecknas av en personlig och exklusiv stil. För att skapa en ett promenadstråk bland träd och musik har en passage skapats med hjälp av en stor upphöjning som inte når ytterkanterna. Mellan slutet av denna L-formade upphöjning av ipe-trä och balkongväggen har man placerat krukor med träd och växter på några stora vita stenar.

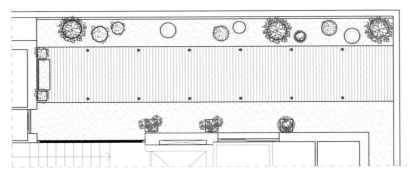

Plan

SUPERPOSITIONS

A low timber fence creates a border for this duplex. The simple but practical play of superimpositions and volumes makes for a peaceful scene. A river of white marble balls was created, from which a timber platform delimits the living area and extends through to the house. At one end there is a custom-made flower bed.

Une petite barrière de planches en bois marque la limite avec la maison mitoyenne. Un ensemble de superpositions et de volumes, simple et pratique, forme un scénario paisible. Une allée de galets de marbre blanc a été créée, surplombée d'une estrade en bois qui délimite la zone de la salle à manger et atteint la maison. À une extrémité, une jardinière en dur avec un parterre de fleurs est mise en valeur.

Ein niedriger Zaun aus Holzlatten bildet die Begrenzung zum Nachbargrundstück. Aus einem ebenso einfachen wie praktischen Spiel von sich überlagernden Formen entsteht ein Ambiente großer Gelassenheit. Ein Fluss aus Marmorkieseln umfließt eine Holzterrasse, die den Essplatz aufnimmt und bis zum Haus reicht. An einem Ende des Hofes wurde ein gemauertes Hochbeet angelegt.

Een laag hek van houten latten vormt de begrenzing van deze geschakelde woning. Het spel met eenvoudige, praktische volumes en superpositie schept een kalme ambiance. Er werd een pad van witte marmersteentjes aangelegd, waarboven een houten loopplank ligt die het eetgedeelte afgrenst en doorloopt tot het huis. Aan één kant trekt een beplante stenen plantenbak de aandacht.

Una valla baja de listones de madera hace de frontera de la vivienda adosada. El juego de superposiciones y volúmenes, sencillo y práctico, conforma un escenario sosegado. Se realizó un río de bolos de mármol blanco del que sobresale una tarima de madera que delimita el área del comedor y llega hasta la casa. En un extremo destaca una jardinera de obra con un parterre de flores.

Una recinzione bassa di listelli di legno funge da limite della casa a schiera. Il gioco di sovrapposizioni e volumi, semplice e pratico, dà forma a uno scenario sereno. È stato concepito un fiume di bocce di marmo bianco dal quale parte un assito di legno che delimita l'area pranzo e arriva fino alla casa. In un'estremità spicca una giardiniera di mattoni con un parterre di fiori.

Uma vedação baixa em ripas de madeira faz a fronteira com o apartamento vizinho. O jogo de sobreposições e volumes, simples e práticos, cria um cenário de tranquilidade. Colocou-se uma fila de colunas em mármore branco a partir da qual se eleva um patamar em madeira a definir a área de refeições que se estende até à casa. Num extremo destaca-se uma floreira em cimento com canteiro de flores.

Ett lågt staket av träribbor fungerar som gräns mot den intilliggande bostaden. Att på ett enkelt och praktiskt sätt stapla och leka med volymer resulterar i en lugn plats. Vita marmorklot placerades på en rad, från vilken en plattform i trä sticker ut och avgränsar matsalen, samt når fram till huset. På ena ytterkanten utmärker sig en specialgjord blomsterrabatt.

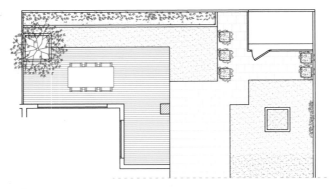

Plan

This patio belongs to the edifice containing the studio of a renowned fashion designer. It is located in the area where private fashion shows are held and used for a place where models, staff, customers and guests can step out for a cigarette. White marble balls boost the natural lighting and an Ipe timber platform extends into a zone with benches, ashtrays and plants.

Cette cour appartient au bâtiment où sont situés les ateliers d'une créatrice de mode connue. Elle se situe dans la zone du *showroom* et des défilés privés et sert d'espace de détente où mannequins, employés, clients et invités sortent fumer. Des galets en marbre blanc renforcent la lumière naturelle et une passerelle en bois d'ipé s'étend dans un espace avec des bancs, des cendriers et des plantes.

Dieser Hof gehört zum Anwesen einer bekannten Modedesignerin. Er liegt gleich neben dem *Showroom* für private Modenschauen und dient in erster Linie als Erholungsbereich für Models und Mitarbeiter, Kunden und Freunde des Hauses. Die weißen Marmorkiesel verstärken das Tageslicht. Der Steg aus Ipe-Holz erweitert sich zu einem Sitzplatz mit Bänken, Pflanzen und Aschenbechern.

Deze patio hoort bij het gebouw met ateliers van een bekende modeontwerpster. Hij ligt bij de ruimte voor privémodeshows en de showroom en wordt gebruikt als ontspanningsruimte waar modellen, medewerkers, klanten en genodigden even kunnen roken. Witmarmeren stenen versterken het daglicht en een loopplank van ipéhout loopt breed uit naar een gedeelte waar banken, asbakken en planten staan.

Este patio pertenece al edificio de talleres de una conocida diseñadora de moda. Se encuentra en la zona de *showroom* y de desfiles privados y es utilizado como área de descanso a la que modelos, trabajadores, clientes e invitados salen a fumar. Unos bolos de mármol blanco potencian la luz natural y una pasarela de madera de ipé se amplía en un espacio con bancos, ceniceros y plantas.

Questo cortile appartiene all'edificio in cui si trovano gli atelier di una nota stilista; attiguo alla zona di *showroom* e di sfilate private, è usato come area di riposo in cui le modelle, i dipendenti, i clienti e gli ospiti escono a fumare. Alcune sfere di marmo bianco sottolineano la luce naturale e una passerella di ipè scorre in uno spazio caratterizzato da panchine, posacenere e piante.

Este pátio pertence ao prédio de andares de uma conhecida desenhadora de moda. Encontra-se na zona de *showroom* e desfiles privados e é utilizado como área de descanso onde modelos, trabalhadores, clientes e convidados podem fumar. Umas colunas de mármore branco intensificam a luz natural e uma passarela em madeira de ipé cresce sobre um espaço com bancos, cinzeiros e plantas.

Den här innergården tillhör en välkänd modedesigners ateljé. Den ligger bland "showrooms" och rum för privata modevisningar, och används som viloutrymme där modeller, arbetare, kunder och gäster går ut och röker. Några vita marmorklot förstärker dagsljuset, och en gångbro i ipe- trä övergår i ett bredare utrymme med bänkar, askfat och växter.

The courtyard of this house was designed as a further inhabitable space. The main goal was to expand the useable area and enjoy it through to the garden, where a barbeque was positioned in one corner next to an outdoor living zone. Thinking of harmony, the ground the courtyard sits on was covered with small stones. An artificial pond completes the outdoor space.

La cour de cette maison a été conçue comme une pièce à vivre de plus. Le principal objectif a été d'étendre l'espace utilisé jusqu'au jardin, où un barbecue a été installé dans un des coins, près du séjour extérieur. Dans une optique d'harmonie, le terrain qui occupe la cour a été recouvert de petites pierres. Un bassin artificiel complète l'espace extérieur.

Der Hof dieses Hauses wurde als ein weiterer Wohnraum eingeplant. Der Raum bis zum Garten sollte so gut wie möglich ausgenutzt werden. In einer Ecke im hinteren Teil des Gartens befindet sich ein Grillplatz mit einem Aufenthaltsbereich. Um das Ambiente des Patios besonders harmonisch zu gestalten, wurde der Boden mit kleinen Steinen bedeckt und ein kleiner Teich angelegt.

De patio van dit huis wordt gezien als extra woonruimte. Hoofddoel was de gebruiksruimte van het huis uit te breiden tot de tuin, waar een barbecue in een van de hoeken werd geplaatst, naast een zitje buiten. Ter wille van de harmonie werd het oppervlak van de patio bedekt met kleine stenen. Een vijver completeert de buitenruimte.

El patio de esta casa fue concebido como una pieza habitable más. El principal objetivo fue extender el espacio de uso y disfrute hasta el jardín, donde se incorporó una barbacoa en una de las esquinas junto una zona de estar exterior. Pensando en la armonía, el terreno que ocupa el patio fue cubierto de pequeñas piedras. Un estanque artificial completa el espacio exterior.

Il cortile di questa casa è stato concepito come una zona abitabile. Lo scopo principale era ampliare lo spazio utile fino al giardino, in un angolo del quale è stato posto un barbecue accanto a un soggiorno esterno. Per ottenere un perfetto equilibrio, il terreno che occupa il cortile è stato coperto di piccole pietre. Un laghetto artificiale completa lo scenario di questo spazio esterno.

O pátio desta casa foi concebido para se tornar mais um espaço habitável. O principal objectivo foi ampliar a área útil e desfrutar do jardim onde, num dos cantos junto a uma zona de estar exterior, se incorporou um churrasco. Pensando em harmonia, o terreno que ocupa o pátio foi coberto de pedras pequenas. Um tanque artificial completa o arranjo deste espaço exterior.

Det här husets innergård var tänkt som ytterligare ett beboeligt utrymme. Det huvudsakliga syftet var att utvidga utrymmet till att nå till trädgården, där man valde att ha en grillplats i ett hörn intill ett yttre vardagsrum. Man tänkte på harmoni när man täckte marken i innergården med små stenar. En konstgjord damm fulländar uterummet.

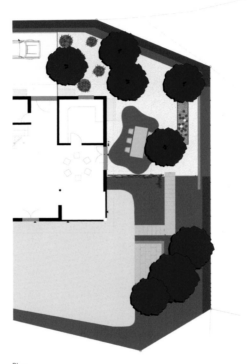

Plan

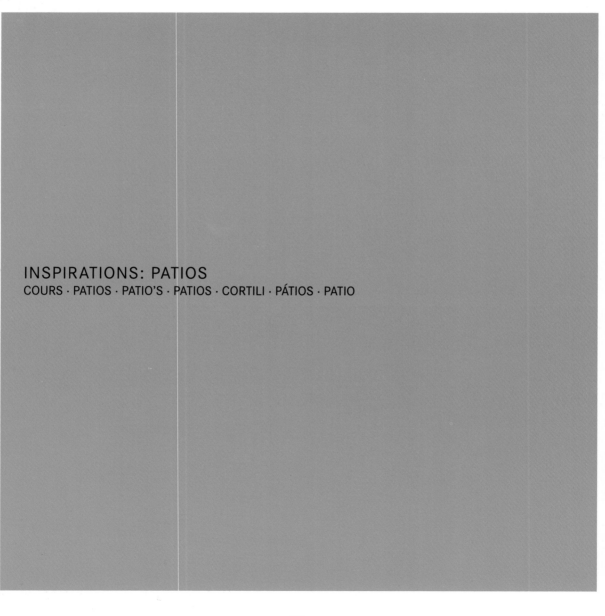

INSPIRATIONS: PATIOS

COURS · PATIOS · PATIO'S · PATIOS · CORTILI · PÁTIOS · PATIO

ROOF GARDENS

TOITS-JARDINS · DACHGÄRTEN · DAKTERRASSEN · CUBIERTAS AJARDINADAS · GIARDINI PENSILI ·
COBERTURAS AJARDINADAS · TAKTERRASSER

If all the flat roofs of a city's buildings could be partially or fully covered in plants, the urban covering would be green. One of the important reasons for opting to build a green roof is to combat the heat-island effect. A traditional building absorbs radiation from the sun and later emits it in the form of heat, making cities at least 4°C hotter than non-built up areas. Roofgardens are an alternative in heavily urbanized cities with little space for green zones and a form of urban landscaping and environmental improvement.

Si toutes les terrasses des bâtiments d'une ville pouvaient être partiellement ou totalement recouvertes de végétation, la toiture urbaine serait verte. Une des raisons importantes qui motive le choix de construire un toit vert est la lutte contre l'effet des îlots de chaleur urbains. Un bâtiment classique absorbe le rayonnement solaire et l'émet ensuite sous forme de chaleur, ce qui donne aux villes des températures supérieures d'au moins 4 °C. Les toits-jardins sont une alternative dans les villes très denses, avec peu d'espace pour des zones vertes, et une forme de naturalisation urbaine et d'amélioration de l'environnement.

Wenn alle Flachdächer ganz oder teilweise begrünt werden könnten, sähen unsere Städte von oben grün aus. Einer der wichtigsten Beweggründe für die Dachbegrünung ist die Bekämpfung des Effekts der Wärmeinsel: Ein in herkömmlicher Bauweise errichtetes Gebäude nimmt die Sonneneinstrahlung auf und gibt sie danach als Wärme wieder ab, sodass in großen Städten in der Regel eine mindestens vier Grad höhere Temperatur als auf dem Land herrscht. Dachgärten sind daher für dicht bebaute Städte mit wenig Grünflächen eine gute Alternative, um die Umweltbedingungen zu verbessern und mehr Natur in die Stadt zu holen.

Als alle dakterrassen op de gebouwen van een stad deels of volledig van vegetatie konden worden voorzien, zou het stedelijke dak groen zijn. Een belangrijke reden om te kiezen voor een groen dak is dat de begroeiing voorkomt dat het dak te heet wordt. Een traditioneel gebouw absorbeert al het zonlicht en stoot het weer als warmte af, waardoor de temperatuur in steden met minstens 4 °C stijgt. Daktuinen zijn een goed alternatief voor steden waarin dicht op elkaar gebouwd is en waar weinig groene ruimte is. Ze zorgen voor een vleugje natuur in de stad en voor een verbeterd milieu.

Si todas las azoteas de los edificios de una ciudad pudieran cubrirse parcial o totalmente de vegetación, el techo urbano sería verde. Una de las principales razones para optar por la construcción de un techo verde es combatir el efecto de isla de calor. Un edificio tradicional absorbe la radiación solar y la emite después en forma de calor, por eso en las ciudades la temperatura suele ser 4 °C más elevada que en el campo. Las cubiertas ajardinadas son una alternativa en poblaciones muy densas con poco espacio para zonas verdes y una forma de paisajismo urbano y de mejora medioambiental.

Se i tetti degli edifici di una città fossero ricoperti, anche parzialmente, di vegetazione, l'intera superficie urbana sarebbe verde. Uno dei motivi più importanti per decidere di costruire una copertura verde è l'effetto isola di calore: gli edifici tradizionali assorbono le radiazioni solari e le restituiscono sotto forma di calore, aumentando di almeno 4 °C la temperatura delle città. I giardini pensili sono un'ottima alternativa in centri caratterizzati da un'elevata concentrazione edilizia e con poche zone verdi; costituiscono anche una buona forma di naturazione urbana e di miglioramento ambientale.

Se todos os telhados dos prédios de uma cidade pudessem ser parcial ou totalmente cobertos de vegetação, o tecto urbano seria verde. Um dos grandes argumentos para optar pela construção de um tecto verde é combater a concentração do calor. Um edifício tradicional absorve a radiação solar e emite-a sob a forma de calor, causando uma elevação de pelo menos 4 °C na temperatura de uma cidade. As coberturas ajardinadas constituem uma alternativa em grandes cidades com pouco espaço para zonas verdes, pois são uma forma de tornar a paisagem urbana menos artificial e de contribuir para um meio ambiente melhor.

Om alla tak täcktes helt eller delvis med växter skulle staden se grön ut ovanifrån. En bra anledning till varför ett grönt tak är att föredra är att det bidrar till att sänka stadstemperaturen. En traditionell byggnad absorberar solenergi och avger sedan värme, vilket gör att städernas temperatur höjs med minst 4 °C. Takterrasser med växtlighet är ett alternativ i tätbebyggda städer där det finns begränsat utrymme för gröna områden. Takterrasser för också in naturen i staden samt bidrar till en bättre miljö.

LICHTBLAU.WAGNER
www.lichtblauwagner.com
© Bruno Klomfar

It was decided to take advantage of the slope of the land and partially bury the house in it to ensure a minimum impact on the landscape. An organic roof helps hide the home and makes it appear an extension of the surroundings. A building well divides the interior into two symmetrical sections, each of which is in turn divided into common areas and bedrooms, with shared services in the middle.

Conçue dans l'idée de tirer profit de la pente du terrain, cette maison est partiellement enterrée afin de réduire au minimum l'impact sur le paysage. Une toiture organique aide à dissimuler la maison en suggérant qu'elle est le prolongement des environs. Un puits de lumière divise l'intérieur en deux parties symétriques, chacune étant divisée à son tour en zones communes et chambres, avec des toilettes partagées au centre.

Um den Eingriff in die Natur so klein wie möglich zu halten, wurde die Schräglage ausgenutzt und das Haus teilweise in den Hang gebaut. Durch das Gründach bleibt es dem Blick fast verborgen. Ein Lichthof unterteilt das Innere in zwei symmetrische Bereiche, die wiederum in Gemeinschaftsräume und Schlafzimmer gegliedert sind. Der in der Mitte liegende Sanitärbereich wird gemeinschaftlich genutzt.

Er werd besloten het huis deels te laten opgaan in de helling van het terrein, om het landschap zo min mogelijk aan te tasten. Het huis gaat enigszins schuil onder een organische overkapping, waardoor het een uitbreiding van de omgeving lijkt. Binnen wordt de ruimte door een lichtkoker in twee symmetrische delen opgesplitst, die zijn onderverdeeld in woon- en slaapkamers, met middenin de voorzieningen.

Se decidió aprovechar la pendiente del terreno y enterrar parcialmente la casa en él, con el fin de causar el mínimo impacto en el paisaje. Una cubierta orgánica ayuda a ocultar la vivienda y la hace parecer una extensión del terreno. Un patio de luces divide el interior en dos secciones simétricas, cada una de las cuales se divide a su vez en zonas comunes y dormitorios, con servicios compartidos en el centro.

Per produrre il minore impatto possibile sull'ambiente, si è deciso di sotterrare parzialmente la casa sfruttando una pendenza del terreno: una copertura organica nasconde l'edificio mimetizzandolo nel paesaggio. Un cortile interno divide lo spazio in due sezioni simmetriche, ognuna delle quali è suddivisa a sua volta in zone comuni e camere da letto, con i servizi al centro.

Decidiu-se aproveitar a inclinação do terreno e nele afundar parcialmente a casa, para minimizar o impacto sobre a paisagem. Uma cobertura orgânica facilita o disfarce da vivenda e fá-la parecer uma extensão da natureza em redor. Um pátio interior divide o interior em duas secções simétricas que, por sua vez, se dividem em zonas comuns e quartos de dormir, com áreas comuns partilhadas no centro.

Man tog beslutet att utnyttja markens sluttning och delvis gömma huset där, i syfte att orsaka så lite skada som möjligt i landskapet. Ett organiskt tak hjälper till att dölja bostaden och gör att den ser ut som en förlängning av omgivningen. En innergård med lampor delar av insidan i två symmetriska ytor, som var och en delats upp i gemensamma utrymmen och sovrum, med gemensamt badrum i mitten.

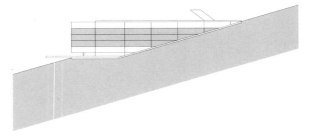

Elevation

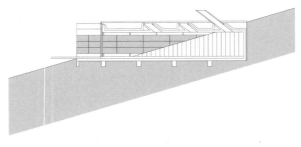

Section

JUNGLE **IN BRONX**

Following the renovation of this 1912 property, the gardened areas on the different levels extend the inhabitable zones and create an emerald world around the house. The top floor has plants such as magnolias, Japanese maples, ornamental apple trees, climbing roses and boxes. On the floor below the plants are the same as those found in a forest: birches, pines and azaleas.

Après la rénovation de cette maison de 1912, les espaces verts des différents niveaux augmentent les zones habitables et créent un monde de couleur émeraude autour de la résidence. À l'étage supérieur, se situent des plantes comme des magnolias, des érables japonais, des pommiers d'ornement, des rosiers grimpeurs et du buis. Un étage en dessous, les plantes sont les mêmes que celles que nous pouvons trouver dans une forêt : bouleau, pin et azalée.

Bei dem Umbau eines Wohnhauses aus dem Jahre 1912 wurden die Wohnräume der verschiedenen Ebenen geschickt durch Gartenbereiche erweitert, die das Haus wie ein grüner Mantel umgeben. Auf der oberen Ebene findet man Pflanzen wie Magnolien, japanischen Ahorn, Zieräpfel, Kletterrosen oder Buchsbaum. Eine Etage tiefer glaubt man, sich im Wald zwischen Birken, Pinien und Azaleen zu befinden.

Na de renovatie van deze woning uit 1912 werden de woongedeelten op de verschillende niveaus uitgebreid met van groen voorziene ruimten, die rondom het huis een smaragdgroene wereld creëren. Op de bovenste verdieping staan o.a. magnolia's, Japanse esdoorn, sierappelbomen, klimrozen en buxus. Een verdieping lager staat vegetatie die we ook in een bos kunnen aantreffen: berk, pijnboom en azalea.

Tras la renovación de esta vivienda de 1912, las estancias ajardinadas en los distintos niveles amplían las zonas habitables y crean un mundo esmeralda a su alrededor. En el piso superior se han plantado magnolias, arces japoneses, manzanos ornamentales, rosales trepadores y bojs. Un piso más abajo, la vegetación es la que podríamos encontrar en un bosque: abedules, pinos y azaleas.

In seguito alla rinnovazione di questa casa del 1912, le zone verdi dei vari piani aumentano il volume delle aree abitabili e creano un mondo smeraldino intorno all'edificio. Al piano superiore si trovano magnolie, aceri giapponesi, meli ornamentali, rose rampicanti e bossi. Al piano sottostante, le piante sono quelle che si potrebbero trovare in un bosco: betulle, pini e azalee.

Após a renovação desta vivenda de 1912, os lugares ajardinados nos diversos níveis aumentaram as áreas habitáveis e criaram um mundo verde-esmeralda a envolver a casa. No andar superior, crescem plantas como magnólias, aceres japoneses, macieiras ornamentais, roseiras trepadoras e buxos. Num piso mais abaixo, encontram-se plantas do ambiente de bosques: vidoeiro, pinheiro e azálea.

Efter renoveringen av denna bostad från 1912 förstorades bostadsytan med hjälp av rummen med trädgårdar på de olika våningarna, vilka även skapar en smaragdfärgad atmosfär kring huset. På övervåningen finns växter som magnolior, japanska lönnträd, dekorativa äppelträd, klättrande rosenbuskar och buxbom. En våning längre ned finns träd som återfinns i skogen: björk, tall och azalea.

JONATHAN LEITERSDORF
© Ian Bradshaw

The city is always present in the background, glimpsed between trees and shrubs. As it if were an oasis, this courtyard is nothing other than a point in space to stop for a moment in the midst of the plants and enjoy the shade of the leafy cover. From the swimming pool, New York unfolds in an uninterrupted 360° view.

La ville est toujours présente au second plan, au loin entre arbres et arbustes. Telle une oasis, cette cour n'est qu'un endroit dans l'espace où nous pouvons nous arrêter un instant au milieu des plantes, afin de profiter de l'ombre de la toiture luxuriante. De la piscine, New York s'étend à perte de vue sur 360°.

In der Ferne, jenseits der Bäume und Sträucher bleibt die Stadt immer sichtbar. Wie in einer Oase fühlt man sich in diesem Dachgarten, an einem Ort, der zum Verweilen einlädt, zur Betrachtung des Grüns, zum Entspannen im Schatten der dichten Pflanzenwelt. Und dann, vom Schwimmbad aus, überrascht einen dieser unglaubliche Rundblick von 360 Grad auf New York.

Half verscholen achter bomen en struiken is de stad altijd op een tweede plan aanwezig. Net als een oase is deze patio een ruimte waar men tussen de planten kan genieten van de schaduw die het weelderige groen biedt. Vanuit het zwembad is in alle richtingen de stad New York te zien.

La ciudad siempre está presente en un segundo plano, vislumbrada entre árboles y arbustos. Como si de un oasis se tratara, este patio no es más que un punto en el espacio donde podemos detenernos por un instante en medio de las plantas y disfrutar la sombra de la frondosa cubierta. Desde la piscina, uno puede disfrutar de una panorámica de Nueva York de 360°.

La città è sempre presente in secondo piano, intravista fra alberi e arbusti. Come se fosse un'oasi, questo cortile non è altro che un punto nello spazio in cui è possibile fermarsi un instante a contemplare la bellezza delle piante all'ombra di una rigogliosa tettoia. Dalla piscina, New York offre un panorama ininterrotto a trecentosessanta gradi.

A cidade permanece em segundo plano, vislumbrada por entre árvores e arbustos. Como se de um oásis se tratasse, este pátio mais não é do que um ponto no espaço, onde podemos deter-nos por instantes no meio de plantas e gozar o prazer da sombra oferecida por frondosa cobertura. Vista da piscina, Nova Iorque expõe-se na continuidade de um círculo de 360°.

Staden är alltid närvarande i bakgrunden, skymd bakom träd och buskar. Som om det vore en oas är den här pation inget annat än en plats där vi kan stanna upp ett ögonblick bland växterna och njuta av skuggan av det lummiga höljet. Från poolen öppnar sig New York oavbrutet i 360°.

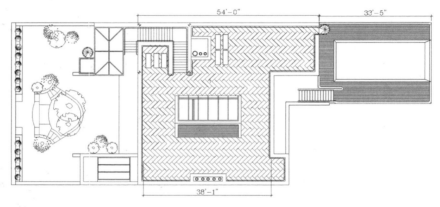

54'-0"

33'-5"

38'-1"

Root plan

GOLF HOLE ON THE ROOFTOP

Building a house with a terrace on top of an industrial building is one way of using the same piece of land twice. If the roof can bear the weight, there is the possibility of creating a garden with an undulating profile. Take it a step further for part of a golf course on the roof of an industrial building. Shrubs at the ends emphasize the nature of this landscape on high.

Construire une maison avec une terrasse sur un bâtiment industriel permet d'utiliser le terrain deux fois. Si la toiture peut supporter le poids, il est possible de créer un jardin au profil ondulé. Avec juste une étape supplémentaire, nous aurons une partie d'un terrain de golf sur le toit d'un bâtiment industriel. Des arbustes à chaque extrémité rehaussent la nature de ce paysage.

Indem man einen Dachgarten auf einem Industriegebäude anlegt, nutzt man das Grundstück sozusagen doppelt. Sofern die Dachkonstruktion ausreichend tragfähig ist, kann sogar ein Garten mit gewelltem Terrain in Betracht gezogen werden. Von dort bis zum Golfplatz ist es dann nur noch ein kleiner Schritt. Schließlich wird mit einer Gehölzgruppe am Rande des Dachs diese „gehobene" Landschaft vollendet.

Door een woning met terras te bouwen op een industrieel gebouw wordt twee keer gebruikgemaakt van een perceel. Als het dak voldoende draagkracht heeft, bestaat de mogelijkheid een glooiende tuin aan te leggen. Nog een stap verder en je beschikt over een stukje golfbaan op het dak van een industrieel gebouw. Enkele struiken aan de kanten zorgen voor een vleugje natuur in dit landschap op hoogte.

Construir una vivienda con terraza sobre un edificio industrial es una forma de utilizar el solar dos veces. Si la cubierta del tejado tiene suficiente capacidad de carga, existe la posibilidad de crear un jardín con un perfil ondulado. Tan sólo un paso más y tendremos parte de un campo de golf en la azotea de un edificio industrial. Unos arbustos en los extremos realzan la naturaleza de este paisaje en lo alto.

Costruire una casa con terrazza su un edificio industriale significa utilizzare l'area edificabile due volte. Se il tetto ha la sufficiente capacità di portata, è possibile creare un giardino con un profilo ondulato e, con qualche sforzo in più, perfino una parte di un campo da golf. Alcuni arbusti nelle parti laterali accrescono l'aspetto naturale di questo paesaggio.

Construir um apartamento com terraço sobre um edifício industrial é duplicar a utilização do terreno. Traçar um jardim de perfil ondulado sobre uma superfície de telhado exige apenas que este tenha capacidade para suportar esse acréscimo de peso. Não tarda que tenhamos um pequeno campo de golfe na açoteia de um edifício industrial. Uns arbustos nos extremos realçam a natureza desta paisagem do alto.

Att bygga en bostad med terrass ovanpå en industribyggnad är ett sätt att använda samma plats två gånger. Om taket är tillräckligt starkt finns möjligheten att skapa en trädgård med en vågig profil. Om man skulle dra det här ett steg längre skulle vi få en golfbana på en industribyggnads takterrass. Några buskar på ytterkanterna framhäver naturen högst upp i detta landskap.

At the top of this old apartment block, a terrace with timber flooring and steel bars evokes the feel of a steamship. One floor below, the climbing plants, steel bars and the pergolas in the courtyards complete the exterior landscape of the building. On the roof, a graphic composition in areas of gravel and succulents acts as a link between the different parts of the garden.

En haut de ce vieil immeuble, une terrasse avec un sol en bois et une grille en acier rappelle l'ambiance à bord d'un bateau à vapeur. Un étage plus bas, les plantes grimpantes, les grilles en acier et les pergolas des cours complètent le paysage extérieur du bâtiment. Sur la toiture, une composition graphique dans des zones avec du gravier et des plantes grasses sert de liaison entre les différentes parties du jardin.

Mit ihrem Holzboden und der Stahlreling erinnert diese Terrasse auf dem Dach eines alten Wohnblocks an das Deck eines Ozeandampfers. Etwas tiefer liegt ein intimerer Bereich mit Stahlgittern, von Pergolen überspannten Patios und Kletterpflanzen. Im Übergangsbereich zwischen den verschiedenen Teilen des Garten ergibt sich ein interessantes Bild aus der Kombination von Kiesschüttung und Sukkulenten.

Boven op dit oude appartementenblok doet het terras met houten vloer en stalen traliewerk denken aan een stoomboot. Een verdieping lager completeren de klimplanten, stalen roosters en pergola's van de patio's de buitenruimte van het gebouw. Op het dak verbindt een grafische compositie de verschillende onderdelen van de tuin met elkaar in een gedeelte met grind en vetplanten.

En lo alto de este viejo bloque de pisos, una terraza con suelo de madera y rejas de acero evoca el ambiente de un barco de vapor. Un piso más abajo, las enredaderas, los enrejados de acero y las pérgolas de los patios completan el paisaje exterior del edificio. En la cubierta, una composición gráfica en zonas de gravilla y suculentas actúa de enlace entre las distintas partes del jardín.

Sopra questo vecchio caseggiato, una terrazza con pavimento di legno e inferriate d'acciaio ricorda l'ambiente di una nave a vapore. Un piano sotto, le piante rampicanti, le grate d'acciaio e le pergole dei cortili coronano il paesaggio esterno dell'edificio. Sul tetto, una composizione grafica a zone di ghiaia e succulente funziona come trait d'union tra le diverse parti del giardino.

No cimo deste velho prédio de andares, um terraço com chão de madeira e grades de metal evoca o ambiente de um barco a vapor. A um nível inferior, as trepadeiras, as grades de ferro e as pérgulas de outros pátios completam a paisagem que envolve o edifício. Na cobertura, uma composição gráfica com zonas de seixos e suculentas cria a união entre as áreas distintas do jardim.

Högst upp i den här gamla lägenhetsbyggnaden frammanas en ångbåtsmiljö med hjälp av en terrass med trägolv och aluminiumgaller. En våning längre ner kompletterar klätterväxterna, spjälverken och innergårdarnas pergolor byggnadens yttre landskap. På taket fungerar en grafisk komposition i grusområdet och suckulenter som länk mellan trädgårdens olika delar.

Plan

STUDIEBUREAU GROENPLANNING BVBA
www.groenplanning.be
© Guy Goethals

The visual style of this loft extends through to the terrace so that interior and exterior come together in a single entity. The main garden elements are made from simple materials like wood, stone and glass, combined with grass and water. At one side, partitions offer an open view across the city. Among the high grass, the water and lawn form an intersection toward the center of the garden.

Le style visuel de ce loft s'étend jusqu'à la terrasse afin que l'intérieur et l'extérieur convergent en une seule entité. Les principaux éléments du jardin sont des matériaux simples comme le bois, la pierre et le verre, combinés à de l'herbe et de l'eau. Sur un des côtés, des parois offrent une vue dégagée sur la ville. Les hautes herbes, l'eau et le gazon forment une intersection vers la moitié du jardin.

Die Terrasse diese Penthouses wurde so angelegt, dass Drinnen und Draußen optisch zusammenfließen. Die Gestaltungselemente sind sehr einfach: Holz, Stein und Glas, kombiniert mit Gräsern und Wasser. An einer Seite gibt der Windschutz den Blick auf die Stadt frei. In der Mitte des Gartens bilden Wasser und Rasen zwischen den hohen Gräsern einen Einschnitt.

De visuele stijl van deze loft loopt door in het terras, waardoor interieur en exterieur tot een eenheid worden. De belangrijkste elementen in de tuin zijn eenvoudige materialen als hout, steen en glas, gecombineerd met gras en water. Aan een van de zijden heeft men via een schuifwand vrij uitzicht over de stad. Tussen de hoge planten vormen water en gazon een snijpunt halverwege de tuin.

El estilo visual de este *loft* se extiende a la terraza de forma que el interior y el exterior constituyen una sola entidad. Los principales elementos del jardín son materiales sencillos como la madera, la piedra y el cristal, combinados con hierba y agua. En uno de los laterales, unas mamparas ofrecen una vista abierta sobre la ciudad. Entre las altas hierbas, el agua y el césped forman una intersección hacia la mitad del jardín.

Lo stile visivo di questo *loft* ha ispirato anche la terrazza, così l'interno e l'esterno formano una sola entità. Gli elementi principali del giardino sono materiali semplici quali il legno, la pietra e il vetro, combinati con erba e acqua. Su un lato, alcuni paraventi offrono un'ampia vista della città. L'erba alta, l'acqua e il prato costituiscono un'intersezione circa al centro del giardino.

O estilo da configuração deste *loft* estende-se ao terraço de forma a que o interior e o exterior partilhem uma só identidade. Os principais elementos do jardim usam materiais simples – madeira, pedra e vidro – em união com plantas e água. Num dos lados, uns biombos oferecem uma vista aberta sobre a cidade. As altas plantas, a água e a relva formam uma intersecção a meio do jardim.

Den visuella stilen på detta loft har även nått terrassen på ett sätt som gör att insidan och utsidan flyter samman i en enda enhet. Trädgårdens huvudsakliga element är enkla material som trä, sten och glas, i kombination med gräs och vatten. På en sida ger några skärmar öppen utsikt över staden. Det höga gräset, vattnet och gräsmattan skapar tillsammans en skärningspunkt i trädgårdens mitt.

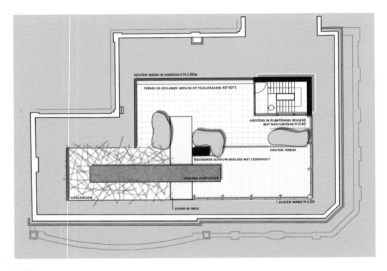

Roof plan

FAINT LIGHT AND **SHADOWS**

PEPE CORTÉS ASOCIADOS
www.pepecortes.es
© Alejandro Bahamón

The designers of this attic were very clear that they wanted a space protected from the sun, with zones of shade and where the light was tenuous. A pergola was built in the southern part, over which climbing plants were left to grow and provide the necessary shade. Different pots with plants were positioned on the northern side of the terrace. The faint light allows the plants to contrast with the wall behind them.

Les concepteurs de ce dernier étage savaient ce qu'ils voulaient : un espace protégé du soleil, avec des zones d'ombre où la lumière soit faible. Sur la partie sud, une pergola a été construite en y laissant pousser des plantes grimpantes, qui fournissent l'ombre nécessaire. Du côté nord de la terrasse, différents pots avec des plantes ont été placés. La lumière faible permet à ces plantes de faire un contraste avec le mur se trouvant derrière elles.

Bei der Gestaltung der Außenbereiche dieses Penthauses musste es vor allem darum gehen, einen Raum im Halbschatten zu schaffen, der vor der Sonne geschützt ist. Daher wurde auf der Südseite eine berankte Pergola errichtet, die den gewünschten Effekt hat. Auf der Nordseite wurden Kübelpflanzen aufgestellt, deren Schatten an der hellen Wand hinter ihnen interessante Effekte erzielen.

De ontwerpers van deze bovenste verdieping wilden een plek die afgeschermd was van de zon, met schaduwpartijen en gedempt licht. Aan de zuidkant werd een pergola gebouwd, waartegen klimplanten groeien die voor de nodige schaduw zorgen. Aan de noordzijde van het terras kwamen bloempotten met verschillende planten te staan. Door het gedempte licht contrasteren deze planten met de muur erachter.

Los diseñadores de este ático tenían muy claro que querían un espacio protegido del sol, con zonas de sombra y donde la luz fuera tenue. En la parte sur se construyó una pérgola sobre la que dejaron crecer enredaderas, que proporcionan la sombra necesaria. En el lado norte de la terraza se colocaron diferentes macetas con plantas. La luz tenue permite que estas plantas contrasten con la pared que se encuentra tras ellas.

I decoratori di questo attico erano sicuri di volere uno spazio riparato dal sole, con zone d'ombra e luce tenue. Nella parte sud è stata costruita una pergola lungo la quale sono state fatte crescere rampicanti, che danno ombra. Sul lato nord della terrazza sono stati installati diversi vasi con piante. La luce tenue fa sì che queste piante creino un contrasto con la parete dietro di esse.

Os criadores deste apartamento num último andar queriam um espaço protegido do sol, com zonas de sombra e luz ténue. Na parte sul, construi-se uma pérgula sobre a qual se deixaram crescer trepadeiras para proporcionar a sombra necessária. No lado norte do terraço, foram colocados diferentes vasos com plantas. A claridade ténue permite a silhueta de contraste destas plantas sobre a parede que se encontra por detrás.

Designerteamet hade mycket klart för sig att de ville ha ett utrymme som var skyddat från solen, med skuggiga områden och där ljuset utomhus är svagt. På den södra delen byggdes en pergola där man lät klätterväxter klänga, vilket ger den skugga som behövs. På den norra sidan av terrassen placerades olika krukväxter. Det svaga ljuset gör att dessa växter kontrasterar mot väggen bakom.

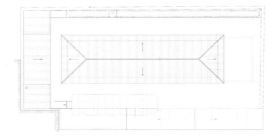

Roof plan

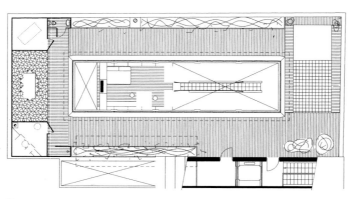

Plan

The garden has a fundamental role in this hotel where the oldest parts date back to 1890. Access to the garden is limited, but from their rooms guests enjoy the view of the flowerbeds with motifs, the path routes and the artfully pruned hedges. When the extension with the swimming pool was added, the roof was used to boost the green space.

Le jardin joue un rôle fondamental dans cet hôtel, dont les parties les plus anciennes remontent à 1890. L'accès au jardin est limité mais, depuis leurs chambres, les hôtes peuvent profiter de la vue des motifs des parterres, du tracé des sentiers et de l'art de la taille des arbustes. Lors de l'agrandissement et de l'ajout de la piscine, la toiture a été utilisée afin de ne pas perdre d'espace vert.

Die ältesten Teile dieses Hotels stammen noch aus dem Jahr 1890. Der Garten macht einen Teil seines besonderen Charmes aus. Obwohl der Zugang eingeschränkt ist, genießen die Hotelgäste aus ihren Zimmern doch den Blick auf die Zierbeete, den Wegverlauf und die kunstvoll beschnittenen Heckensträucher. Bei der Anlage eines Schwimmbeckens wurde das Dach bepflanzt, um keinen Meter Grünfläche zu verlieren.

In dit hotel, waarvan de oudste gedeelten uit 1890 stammen, speelt de tuin een essentiële rol. Er is beperkte toegang tot de tuin, maar de gasten kunnen vanuit hun kamer genieten van de motieven in de bloembedden, de figuren van de paden en de kunstig gesnoeide struiken. Toen er een uitbreiding met zwembad kwam, werd het dak gebruikt, zodat geen groene ruimte verloren zou gaan.

El jardín tiene un papel fundamental en este hotel, cuyas partes más antiguas se remontan a 1890. El acceso al jardín está limitado, pero desde sus habitaciones los huéspedes pueden disfrutar de la vista de los motivos de los parterres, el trazado de las veredas y los setos recortados. Cuando se añadió la ampliación con la piscina, la cubierta fue utilizada para que no se perdiera espacio verde.

Sebbene abbia un accesso limitato, il giardino svolge un ruolo fondamentale in questo albergo, le cui parti più antiche risalgono al 1890. Dalle loro stanze, gli ospiti possono ammirare i motivi creati dai parterre, dal tracciato dei sentieri e dall'arte della potatura degli arbusti. Quando si aggiunse l'annesso con la piscina, la copertura fu utilizzata in modo da non perdere spazio verde.

O jardim tem um papel fundamental neste hotel, cujas áreas mais antigas remontam a 1890. O acesso ao jardim é limitado mas, dos seus aposentos, os hóspedes podem desfrutar da vista sobre os motivos dos canteiros, o traçado das alamedas e a arte da poda de arbustos. Com as obras de ampliação e da piscina, recorreu-se à cobertura para criar um espaço verde que diminuísse a perda do anterior.

Trädgården spelar en grundläggande roll i det här hotellet, vars äldsta delar härrör från 1890. Tillgången till trädgården har begränsats, men från rummen kan gästerna njuta av utsikten över blomsterrabatternas motiv, stigarnas skiss och de beskurna buskarnas konstverk. När man skapade utbyggnaden med poolen använde man sig av taket för att man inte skulle gå miste om det gröna.

KOEN ROBBERECHT PLANTENDIENST
www.koenrobberecht.be
© Guy Obijn

This garden is ideal for sitting down and enjoying in the morning or evening. The climbers, low plants, and flowers create a matchless natural environment on the top of the home. A small pond between the two terraces further intensifies this impression. From the terrace, the warmth of the old city is seen, with monuments such as the opera house, the towers and the innumerable roofs.

Ce jardin est idéal pour s'asseoir et pour en profiter aussi bien le matin que le soir. Les plantes grimpantes, celles de faible hauteur et les fleurs créent un environnement naturel incomparable en haut de la maison. Un petit bassin situé entre les deux terrasses accentue davantage cette impression. À partir de la terrasse, il est possible de percevoir la chaleur de la ville ancienne avec des monuments comme l'Opéra, les tours et les toits à perte de vue.

Die Stimmung in diesem Garten genießt man am besten in den frühen Morgen- oder späten Abendstunden. Kletterpflanzen, halbhohe Gewächse und Blumen schaffen ein unvergleichliches Ambiente über dem Wohnhaus. Der Eindruck der Natürlichkeit wird verstärkt von einem kleinen Teich zwischen den zwei Terrassen. Von hier oben fällt der Blick auf die altehrwürdige Stadt mit der Oper, den Türmen und der Vielfalt der Dächer.

Deze tuin is ideaal om 's ochtends of 's avonds lekker in te zitten. De klimplanten, de laagblijvende planten en de bloemen scheppen een ongeëvenaarde natuurlijke omgeving boven op de woning. Een kleine vijver tussen de twee terrassen versterkt deze indruk nog. Vanaf het terras is de gloed van de oude stad waarneembaar, met monumenten als de Opera, hoge torens en een zee van daken.

La primera hora de la mañana y el atardecer son los mejores momentos para disfrutar de este jardín. Las enredaderas, las plantas de poca altura y las flores crean un entorno natural inigualable en lo alto de la vivienda. Un pequeño estanque situado entre las dos terrazas intensifica aún más esta impresión. Desde la terraza, se percibe la calidez de la antigua ciudad con monumentos como la Ópera, las torres y la infinidad de tejados.

I momenti migliori per ammirare la bellezza di questo giardino sono il mattino e la sera. Le piante rampicanti, gli arbusti bassi e i fiori sul tetto creano un ambiente naturale ineguagliabile, che è reso ancor più attraente da un laghetto tra le due terrazze. Da questo luogo, è sorprendente la vista della città vecchia con i suoi monumenti quali l'Opera, le torri e l'infinita estensione dei tetti.

Este jardim é o espaço ideal, seja de manhã ou à tarde, para se sentar com prazer. As trepadeiras, as plantas baixas e as flores criam um ambiente natural inigualável no cimo da vivenda. Um pequeno lago situado entre os dois terraços torna a impressão mais intensa. Do terraço, percebe-se o calor da antiga cidade com monumentos como a Ópera, as torres e a infinidade de telhados.

Den här trädgården är idealisk för att slå sig ner och njuta i en morgon- eller kvällsmiljö. Klätterväxterna, de lägre växterna och blommorna skapar en enastående naturlig miljö högst upp i bostaden. En liten damm mellan de två terrasserna förstärker detta intryck ännu mer. Från terrassen uppfattar man värmen från den gamla staden, med monument som operahuset, tornen och de oräkneliga taken.

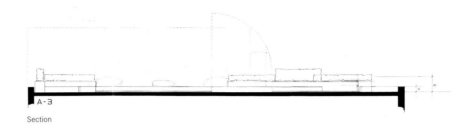

A-Ǝ

Section

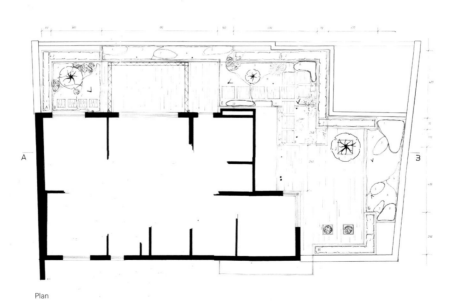

A ⊣   Ǝ

Plan

R. HERMS LANDSCHAFTSARCHITEKT
www.raimundherms.de
© Martin Eberle

One has the impression that nature has completely invaded this school. It seems as though the rocks support the building, but when there is a heavy shower the rainwater is also channeled downward to impregnate the soil. The plants emphasize the ecological nature, signaling the paths and delimiting the spaces where the children play.

On a ici l'impression que la nature a totalement envahi cette école. Les rochers semblent supporter le bâtiment mais, en cas d'averse, ils canalisent aussi l'eau de pluie vers le bas de manière à imprégner le sol. Les plantes se chargent de mettre la nature écologique en valeur, en indiquant les sentiers et en délimitant les espaces où les enfants peuvent jouer à certaines heures.

Hier scheint die Natur in die Schule eingedrungen zu sein. Es sieht so aus, als ob die Felsen das Gebäude trügen, doch sie dienen auch zur Ableitung des Regenwassers, das zur Bewässerung genutzt wird. Gemäß dem ökologischen Naturverständnis sind es die Pflanzen, die den Kindern die Wege weisen und ihnen den Platz zeigen, an dem sie zu bestimmten Zeiten spielen können.

Het is alsof de natuur deze school helemaal is binnengedrongen. De rotsen lijken het gebouw slechts te ondersteunen, maar wanneer er een plensbui valt, leiden ze het regenwater naar beneden, zodat de bodem wordt bevloeid. De planten benadrukken de milieuvriendelijkheid van het gebouw en geven de paden en ruimten aan waar kinderen op gezette tijden kunnen spelen.

Da la impresión de que la naturaleza ha invadido por completo esta escuela. Parece que las rocas soporten el edificio, pero cuando hay un aguacero también canalizan el agua de lluvia hacia abajo de forma que impregne el suelo. Las plantas, que realzan el carácter ecológico del proyecto, sirven para señalar las veredas y delimitar los espacios donde pueden jugar los niños.

Questa scuola sembra invasa completamente dalla natura. È come se le rocce sopportino il peso dell'edificio, ma quando c'è un acquazzone, servono anche per canalizzare l'acqua piovana verso il terreno sottostante. Le piante accrescono la natura ecologica del progetto, definendo i percorsi e delimitando gli spazi in cui i bambini possono giocare.

A impressão é de que a natureza invadiu por completo esta escola. As pedras, que parecem servir de apoio ao edifício, servem também, quando chove, de escoadouro para a água que corre para o solo. As plantas realçam a presença da natureza, assinalando as calçadas e delimitando os espaços em que as crianças podem brincar durante os recreios.

Man får intrycket av att naturen har tagit över den här skolan helt och hållet. Det verkar som om klipporna håller byggnaden uppe, men när det kommer en störtskur leds regnvattnet neråt så att marken suger upp vattnet. Växterna lyfter fram det ekologiska i naturen, genom att de markerar stigarna och avgränsar de utrymmen som är avsedda för lek under bestämda tider.

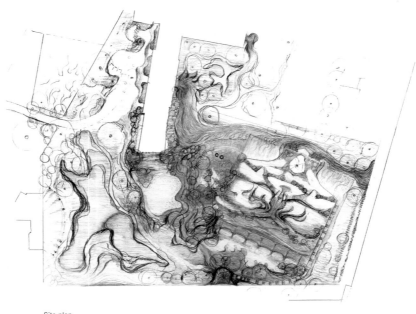

Site plan

CONTRAST AND UNIFORMITY

BART HAVERKAMP & PIETER CROES/GROENDESIGNERS
www.bart-pieter.be
© Guy Obijn

Although the shapes and materials employed form contrasts between them – wood and metal, rigid and organic, terracotta and lead – the overall image of the gardened spaces radiates peace and harmony. The beech hedges that surround each of these spaces create a closed space. In turn, the row of trees brings a sense of calm to this terrace with its zones of sun, shade and water. In spring, the feeling of uniformity is emphasized by the white buds that cover all the planted sections.

Bien que les formes et matériaux utilisés forment un contraste, l'image générale de l'ensemble des jardins diffuse de la tranquillité et de l'harmonie. Les haies de hêtres entourant chacun de ces espaces créent une ambiance fermée. La rangée d'arbres apporte, à son tour, tranquillité à la terrasse avec ses zones d'ombre. Au printemps, la sensation d'uniformité est soulignée par les boutons blancs des fleurs qui couvrent toutes les sections plantées.

Trotz der unterschiedlichen verwendeten Materialien und der Vielfalt der Formen ergibt sich bei diesem Garten ein ruhiges, harmonisches Gesamtbild. Die Buchenhecken verleihen jedem der kleinen Räume Geschlossenheit, und die Baumreihe gibt der Terrasse Ruhe und Schatten. Im Frühling stellt sich die gesamte Anlage noch einheitlicher dar, wenn die Pflanzen ihre weißen Knospen hervorbringen.

Hoewel de vormen en materialen met elkaar contrasteren, straalt het geheel van deze groene ruimten rust en harmonie uit. De hekken van beukenhout rond de verschillende ruimten scheppen een besloten sfeer. Tegelijkertijd zorgt de schaduw van de rij bomen voor rust op het terras. In de lente wordt het gevoel van eenheid nog versterkt door de witte knoppen waarmee alle aangeplante delen zijn bedekt.

A pesar de que las formas y los materiales contrastan entre sí, el conjunto de los espacios ajardinados transmite una imagen general de tranquilidad y armonía. Los setos de haya que rodean cada uno de estos espacios crean un ambiente cerrado. A su vez, la hilera de árboles aporta sosiego a la terraza con sus zonas de sombra. En primavera, la sensación de uniformidad se ve realzada por los capullos blancos que cubren todas las secciones plantadas.

Sebbene le forme e i materiali creino un forte contrasto, l'immagine complessiva diffonde una sensazione di tranquillità e armonia. Le siepi di faggio generano un ambiente chiuso, mitigato però dalla fila d'alberi che, grazie alle sue zone d'ombra, dà alla terrazza un senso di pace. In primavera, l'impressione di uniformità aumenta grazie ai boccioli bianchi che coprono tutte le sezioni coltivate.

Apesar do contraste entre as formas e os materiais, o conjunto das áreas ajardinadas irradia tranquilidade e harmonia. As sebes de faia que rodeiam cada um destes espaços criam pequenos refúgios isolados. Por sua vez, a sombra projectada pela ala de árvores envolve em paz este terraço. Na Primavera, a sensação de harmonia é realçada pelas flores brancas que enfeitam as áreas ajardinadas.

Trots att formerna och materialen skiljer sig från varandra utstrålar den sammanlagda bilden av utrymmena med trädgårdar lugn och harmoni. Bokhäckarna som omger vart och ett av dessa utrymmen skapar en sluten atmosfär. Längan av träd ger på sitt sätt lugn åt terrassen med skuggiga utrymmen. På våren framhävs enhetligheten genom de vita knopparna som täcker alla planterade ytor.

This garden is located on the roof of an industrial building because there was not enough space on the ground for a natural garden. The vegetation has been adapted to a variety of biotopes. The marsh plants, perennial species, the plants typical to rocky environments, the grass and the strong shrubs define the garden's organic character.

Ce jardin se situe sur la toiture d'un bâtiment industriel car il n'y avait pas assez de place au sol pour un jardin naturel. La végétation s'est adaptée à une variété de biotopes. La végétation marécageuse, les espèces persistantes, les plantes d'environnements rocheux, les herbes et les arbustes forts définissent le caractère organique de ce jardin.

Aus Mangel an geeignetem Platz zu ebener Erde wurde der Garten auf dem Dach des Gewerbegebäudes angelegt. Die Bepflanzung ist verschiedenen natürlichen Biotopen nachempfunden: Sumpfvegetation, immergrüne Pflanzen, Felsenbewohner, Kräuter, Gräser und kräftige Sträucher bestimmen den organischen Charakter dieses Gartens.

Deze tuin bevindt zich op het dak van een industrieel gebouw. Beneden was onvoldoende ruimte om een tuin aan te leggen. De vegetatie hoort bij verschillende biotopen. Groenblijvende moerasplanten, planten uit rotsige omgevingen, grassen en struiken bepalen het ecologische karakter van deze tuin.

Este jardín se sitúa en la cubierta de un edificio industrial debido a que no había suficiente espacio en el suelo para un jardín natural. La vegetación se ha adaptado a una variedad de biotopos. La vegetación pantanosa, las especies perennes, las plantas de entornos rocosos, las hierbas y los fuertes arbustos definen el carácter orgánico de este jardín.

Questa zona verde ricopre il tetto di un edificio industriale, giacché intorno non v'era sufficiente spazio per un giardino naturale. La vegetazione è proveniente da diversi biotopi: la flora pantanosa, le specie perenni, le piante di ambienti rocciosi, le erbe e i forti arbusti definiscono il carattere organico di questo giardino.

A razão para este jardim no cimo de um edifício industrial resultou da falta de espaço suficiente para um jardim natural no solo. A vegetação foi adaptada a uma variedade de biotopos. Vegetação pantanosa, espécies perenes, plantas oriundas de zonas rochosas, ervas e arbustos resistentes conferem ao jardim um ar natural.

Den här trädgården återfinns på taket av en industribyggnad, eftersom det inte fanns tillräckligt med utrymme på marken för en naturlig trädgård. Växtligheten har anpassat sig efter ett flertal biotyper. Träskväxterna, perennerna, växterna från bergiga områden, örterna och de starka buskarna definierar den organiska prägeln i denna trädgård.

OPEN AND CLOSED SPACES

JOZEF FEYT & THIERRY DENIS/ALFA GREEN
www.alfagreen.be
© Guy Obijn

The timber structures horizontally and vertically organize this terrace with views over the historical city of Antwerp. The afternoon light is reflected between the wooden boards, creating a relaxed atmosphere at the end of the day. There are different views from the terrace: the roofs, treetops and passersby in the square just below.

Les structures en bois ordonnent tant horizontalement que verticalement cette terrasse avec vue sur la ville historique d'Anvers. L'après-midi, la lumière se reflète entre les lattes en bois, créant ainsi une atmosphère détendue pendant les dernières heures du jour. Le panorama varie depuis la terrasse : les toits, les cimes des arbres ou les passants sur la place se trouvant juste en dessous.

Der Anblick dieser Dachterrasse in der Altstadt von Antwerpen wird von waagerecht und senkrecht verlaufenden Holzstrukturen bestimmt. Nachmittags färbt das Licht der Sonne die Holzleisten ein und vergoldet die Stimmung der letzten Stunden des Tages. Von hier bietet sich eine Vielzahl von Ausblicken: auf die Nachbardächer, die Wipfel der Bäume oder hinunter auf die Passanten auf dem Platz vor dem Haus.

De houten structuren brengen zowel horizontaal als verticaal orde aan op dit terras met uitzicht op het historische deel van Antwerpen. 's Middags valt het licht tussen het houten latwerk door en schept een sfeer van ontspanning in de laatste uren van de dag. Vanaf het terras is er een ander uitzicht: daken, boomtoppen en voorbijgangers op het plein beneden.

Las estructuras de madera ordenan tanto horizontal como verticalmente esta terraza con vistas a la ciudad histórica de Amberes. Por la tarde, la luz se refleja entre los listones de madera creando un ambiente relajado en las últimas horas del día. Las vistas desde la terraza son diversas: los tejados, las copas de los árboles, o los transeúntes de la plaza que se encuentra justo debajo.

Le strutture di legno ordinano in senso tanto orizzontale quanto verticale questa terrazza con vista sul centro storico di Amberes. Al pomeriggio, la luce filtra attraverso i listelli di legno creando un pacifico ambiente vespertino. Dalla terrazza si godono diverse viste: i tetti, le chiome degli alberi o la gente che passa per la piazza sottostante.

Estruturas de madeira regem, tanto horizontal como verticalmente, este terraço com vista sobre a cidade histórica da Antuérpia. Pela tarde, a luz côa-se por entre essas ripas de madeira criando um ambiente repousante nas últimas horas do dia. O olhar debruça-se sobre os telhados, as copas das árvores, os transeuntes da praça localizada exactamente por baixo.

Träkonstruktionerna skapar ordning både horisontellt och vertikalt på den här terrassen med utsikt över den historiska stadskärnan i Amberes. På eftermiddagen filtreras ljuset mellan träribborna, vilket skapar en avslappnad atmosfär under dagens sista timmar. Vyerna från terrassen skiljer sig: taken, trädkronorna, eller förbipasserande på torget precis nedanför.

Plan

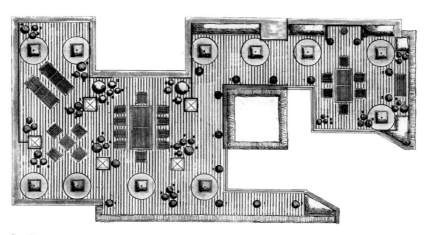

Elevation

MEADOW HOUSE

FILIP ENGELS/GROEN VOOR BEDRIJVEN NV
www.groenvoorbedrijven.be
© Guy Obijn

Set on the roof of a five-storey building, this hanging garden exudes the atmosphere of a 19th-century cabin. The wall with a door, the rustic brick floor of the terrace, the greenhouse, garden furniture and the shed with a pump are in perfect harmony with the plants of yesteryear.

Situé sur la toiture d'un bâtiment de cinq étages, ce jardin suspendu offre l'atmosphère d'une cabane du XIXᵉ siècle. La clôture avec sa porte, le sol de la terrasse en brique rustique, la serre, le mobilier de jardin et l'abri avec une pompe sont en parfaite harmonie avec les plantes d'antan.

Dieser „hängende" Garten befindet sich auf dem Dach eines fünfgeschossigen Hauses und ist einer Laube des 19. Jahrhunderts nachempfunden. Der Zaun mit dem Gartentor, die mit Handstrichziegeln gepflasterte Terrasse, der Wintergarten, die Gartenmöbel und der Schuppen mit der Pumpe stehen im Einklang mit der nostalgischen Bepflanzung.

Deze hangende tuin bevindt zich op het dak van een gebouw van vijf verdiepingen en ademt de sfeer van vroeger eeuwen. De omheining met de deur, de vloer van rustieke tegels op het terras, de serre, de tuinmeubels en de overkapping passen volmaakt bij de planten.

Ubicado en la cubierta de un edificio de cinco plantas, este jardín colgante transmite el ambiente de una cabaña del siglo XIX. La cerca con su puerta, el suelo de la terraza de ladrillo rústico, el invernadero, el mobiliario de jardín y el cobertizo con una bomba armonizan a la perfección con las plantas de antaño.

Situato sul tetto di un edificio di cinque piani, questo giardino pensile offre l'atmosfera di un capanno del XIX secolo. La recinzione con la sua porta, il pavimento di mattoni rustici, la serra, l'arredamento da giardino e la tettoia con pompa, che si usavano una volta, stanno in perfetta armonia con le piante.

Localizado no cimo de um edifício de cinco andares, este jardim suspenso dá a impressão de uma cabana do século XIX. A cerca, e a respectiva porta, o pavimento de ladrilho rústico, a estufa, a mobília de jardim e o alpendre com uma são reprodução perfeita de imagens de outrora.

På taket på en femvåningsbyggnad finns den här hängande trädgården som andas stugmiljö i 1800-talsanda. Staketet med dess dörr, terrassens golv av rustik tegelsten, växthuset, trädgårdsmöblemanget och skärmtaket med vattenledare harmoniserar perfekt med växterna från förr.

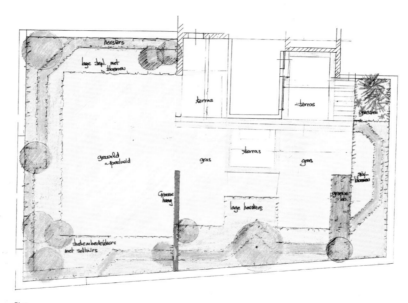

Plan

MIMETIC HOUSE

DOMINIC STEVENS ARCHITECT
www.dominicstevensarchitect.net
© Ros Kavanagh

Mimetic House is a project by Irish architect Dominic Stevens where the goal was to form part of the environment, reflecting it and changing with it during each season of the year. The roof is a flat surface on which the grass and local plants grow. During the day it looks like just another shrub. At night it is only visible when the lights from inside reveal its presence. The materials are all recyclable.

Mimetic House est un projet de l'architecte irlandais Dominic Stevens dont l'objectif est de faire partie de l'environnement, en le reflétant et en changeant avec lui à chaque saison de l'année. Le toit est une surface plate où le gazon et les plantes de la région poussent. Le jour, on dirait un arbuste de plus. La nuit, il est seulement visible quand les lumières de l'intérieur révèlent sa présence. Les matériaux sont tous recyclés.

Mimetic House ist ein Projekt des irischen Architekten Dominic Stevens, das darin besteht, das Haus ganz Teil seiner Umgebung werden zu lassen, es den jahreszeitlichen Veränderungen zu unterwerfen. Auf dem flachen Dach wachsen Gras und heimische Pflanzen. Das Haus fällt tagsüber nicht auf, und nachts ist es nur sichtbar, wenn die Lichter es verraten. Alle Baumaterialien sind wieder verwendbar.

Mimetic House is ontworpen door de Ierse architect Dominic Stevens. Doelstelling was dat het huis deel zou uitmaken van de omgeving, deze moest weerspiegelen en met elk jaargetijde mee zou veranderen. Op het dak groeien gras en planten uit de streek. Overdag lijkt het dak een extra stuk omgeving. 's Avonds zie je het alleen als het licht vanbinnen erop schijnt. Er is louter gerecycled materiaal gebruikt.

Mimetic House es un proyecto del arquitecto irlandés Dominic Stevens cuyo objetivo es formar parte del entorno, reflejándolo y cambiando con él cada estación del año. El tejado es una superficie plana donde crece el césped y las plantas de la zona. Durante el día parece un arbusto más. De noche, sólo es visible cuando las luces del interior descubren su presencia. Los materiales son todos reciclados.

Mimetic House è un progetto dell'architetto irlandese Dominic Stevens il cui obiettivo consiste nel far parte dell'ambiente, imitandolo e modificandosi a ogni cambiamento di stagione. Il tetto è una superficie piatta su cui crescono il prato e le piante della zona: di giorno sembra un arbusto tra gli altri, e di notte, è visibile solo quando le luci dell'interno ne rivelano la presenza. I materiali sono tutti riciclati.

Mimetic House, um projecto do arquitecto irlandês Dominic Stevens, pretende uma integração total no ambiente, reflectindo-o e acompanhando a sua mudança ao longo das estações do ano. O telhado é uma superfície plana onde crescem erva e plantas locais. Durante o dia lembra um arbusto mais, à noite deixa-se ver apenas quando se acendem as luzes no interior. Todos os materiais são reciclados.

Mimetic House är ett projekt av den irländske arkitekten Dominic Stevens, där syftet var att integrera bostaden i omgivningen, och på så sätt återspegla miljön och förändras efter varje årstid. Taket är en jämn yta där gräsmattan och växter från trakten frodas. Under dagen ser det ut som ännu en buske. På natten syns det bara när ljusen inifrån avslöjar dess närvaro. Allt material är återanvänt.

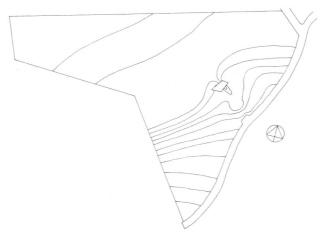

Site plan

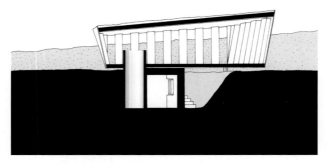

Section

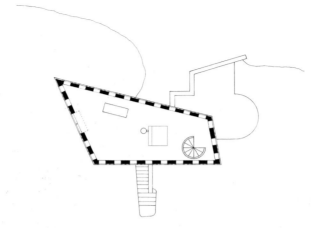

Plan

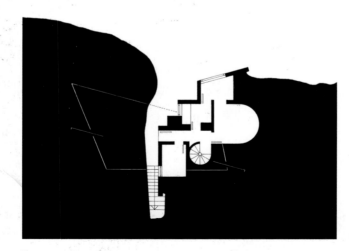

Plan

BERT LENS/LENS ASS ARCHITECTEN
www.lensass.be
© Guy Obijn

There is no hierarchy between the elements of the roof of this building, an old workshop. The clean lines of the floor, walls, table and chairs were designed by the owner. The color white, the choice of the architect, dominates the space. The old part of the city, with its towers and innumerable roofs, becomes an integral part of this roofgarden. Seen from up high, the landscape unfolds at cornice level.

Il n'existe aucune hiérarchie entre les éléments de la toiture de ce bâtiment, un ancien atelier. Le sol, les murs, la table et les sièges sont de fabrication propre et leurs lignes sont simples. La couleur blanche, choisie par l'architecte, domine l'espace. La partie ancienne de la ville, avec ses tours et sa multitude de toits, devient une partie intégrante de cette terrasse. Vu d'en haut, le paysage s'étend au niveau de la corniche.

Dieser Dachgarten auf einem ehemaligen Werkstattgebäude wurde mit einfachen, selbst gefertigten Elementen gestaltet, die sich perfekt ergänzen: Boden, Wände, Tisch und Stühle. Auf Wunsch des Architekten herrscht weiß vor. Die Altstadt mit ihrer Vielzahl von Türmen und Dächern wird zu einem integralen Bestandteil der Dachterrasse: Die Stadtlandschaft dehnt sich hier zu Füßen des Betrachters aus.

Er is geen enkele hiërarchie tussen de elementen op het dak van deze voormalige werkplaats. De vloer, wanden, tafel en zitjes zijn eenvoudig van lijn en zelfgemaakt. De kleur wit, een keuze van de architect, domineert de ruimte. Het oude stadsdeel, met zijn hoge gebouwen en zee van daken, maakt deel uit van dit dakterras. Van bovenaf gezien bevindt de omgeving zich op het niveau van de deklijst.

No existe ninguna jerarquía entre los elementos de la cubierta de este edificio, un antiguo taller. El suelo, las paredes, la mesa y los asientos, de líneas simples, han sido diseñados por el propietario. El color blanco, elección del arquitecto, domina el espacio. La parte antigua de la ciudad, con sus torres e infinidad de tejados, se convierten en parte integrante de esta azotea. Visto desde lo alto, el paisaje se despliega al nivel de la cornisa.

Tra gli elementi del tetto di questo edificio, un vecchio laboratorio, non vi è alcuna gerarchia. Il pavimento, le pareti, il tavolo e i sedili, dalle linee semplici, sono artigianali. Il colore bianco, una scelta dell'architetto, domina lo spazio. La città vecchia, che scorre a livello del cornicione, con le sue torri e l'infinita estensione di tetti, diviene un elemento in più di questa copertura.

Não existe qualquer hierarquia entre os elementos do espaço, uma antiga oficina, no cimo deste edifício. O chão, as paredes, a mesa e os assentos são de fabrico artesanal e de linhas simples. O branco, escolha do arquitecto, domina o espaço. A parte antiga da cidade, com torres e múltiplos telhados, torna-se parte integrante desta açoteia. Vista do alto, a paisagem exibe-se ao nível da cornija.

Det råder ingen hierarkisk ordning bland inslagen på taket av den här byggnaden- en gammal verkstad. Golv, väggar, bord och stolar har designats av ägaren och har enkla linjer. Den vita färgen, vald av arkitekten, dominerar i utrymmet. Den gamla delen av staden, med dess torn och otaliga tak, integreras med denna takterrass. Sett från ovan breder landskapet ut sig i jämnhöjd med kornischerna.

Plan

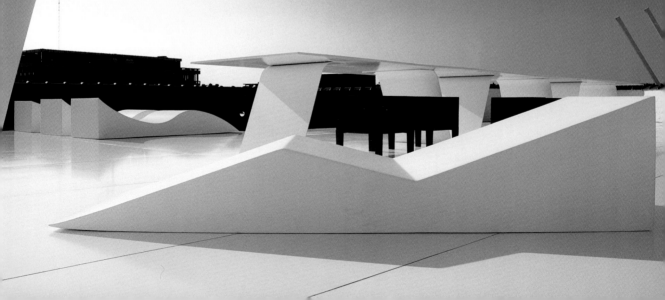

ARBORÈTUM
www.arboretum.es
© Jordi Jové

The access to the terrace of this family home is via the main bedroom. The well-appointed space features a gym, a spa area and a sauna. The terrace was designed to complete this relaxation area in which all the elements are arranged to guarantee wellbeing outside of the property.

L'accès à la terrasse de cette maison familiale se fait par la pièce principale. Cette luxueuse pièce dispose d'un gymnase, d'un spa et d'un sauna. La terrasse a été conçue pour compléter cet espace de détente et tous les éléments sont disposés de façon à garantir le bien-être à l'extérieur de la maison.

Über das Schlafzimmer der Eigentümer gelangt man auf die Terrasse dieses Einfamilienhauses. Das luxuriös ausgestattete Anwesen verfügt über einen Fitnessraum, einen Spa-Bereich und eine Sauna. Die Terrasse, auf der alles auf das Wohlfühlen und Entspannen unter freiem Himmel ausgerichtet ist, ergänzt diese Annehmlichkeiten vorzüglich.

Het terras van deze eengezinswoning is via de ouderslaapkamer te bereiken. De luxeuze ruimte heeft een fitnessgedeelte, een spa en een sauna. Om de ontspanningsruimte te completeren werd het terras ontworpen. Daarin zijn alle elementen aanwezig voor een aangenaam vertoeven buiten de woning.

El acceso a la terraza de esta vivienda unifamiliar se realiza a través del dormitorio principal. La lujosa habitación dispone de gimnasio, zona de *spa* y sauna. Para completar esta área de relajación se diseñó la terraza, en la que todos los elementos están dispuestos para garantizar el bienestar fuera de la vivienda.

L'accesso alla terrazza di questa abitazione unifamiliare avviene attraverso la camera da letto principale. La lussuosa stanza è dotata di palestra, zona *spa* e sauna. Per completare tale area di relax è stata progettata la terrazza, sulla quale ogni elemento è disposto in modo tale da garantire tutte le comodità anche all'esterno della casa.

O acesso ao terraço desta vivenda unifamiliar processa-se através do quarto principal. O aposento de luxo dispõe de ginásio, zona de *spa* e sauna. Para completar esta área de descontracção foi desenhado um terraço, no qual todos os elementos se encontram dispostos de forma a proporcionarem bem-estar no exterior da habitação.

I det här enfamiljshuset kommer man till terrassen genom det stora sovrummet. Gym, spa- avdelning och bastu finns i det lyxiga rummet. För att detta avslappningsutrymme skulle fulländas skapades terrassen, där samtliga delar syftar till att uppnå välbefinnande även utomhus.

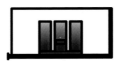

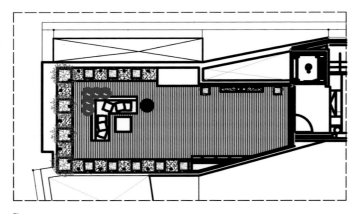

Plan

One of the major challenges of this project involved integrating the different levels next to the swimming pool. Roof pools are built on a raised platform. One side of this platform was used as the back of a long sofa in the chill-out space, while a solarium with direct access to the pool was designed on the other side.

L'un des grands défis de ce projet a été d'adapter les différents niveaux à une piscine. Une piscine située sur le toit d'un immeuble est le plus souvent construite sur une estrade. L'un des côtés de cette plate-forme a été utilisé comme dossier pour un grand canapé de la zone *chill-out*. De l'autre côté, un solarium a été installé avec accès à la piscine.

Die größte gestalterische Herausforderung bei der Anlage dieser Terrasse bestand in der Kombination eines Schwimmbeckens und mehrerer Ebenen. Wasserbecken auf Dachterrassen werden in der Regel erhöht in einem Podest angelegt. Hier wurde eine der Seiten dieses Podests als Rückenlehne für das Sofa des Chill-out-Bereichs genutzt. Auf der anderen Seite entstand eine Sonnenterrasse mit Stufen zum Pool.

Een uitdaging van dit project vormde de integratie van de hoogteverschillen rond het zwembad. Zwembaden boven op gebouwen worden op een verhoogd platform aangelegd. Van een van de zijden van dit platform werd de rugleuning van een grote bank in de *chill-out*-ruimte gemaakt. Aan de andere kant kwam een zonneterras met toegang tot het zwembad.

Uno de los grandes retos de este proyecto fue integrar los diferentes niveles junto a la piscina. Las piscinas construidas en las cubiertas de los edificios se construyen sobre una tarima elevada. Uno de los laterales de esta plataforma se aprovechó como respaldo de un largo sofá de la zona del *chill-out*. Al otro lado, se diseñó un solárium con acceso directo a la piscina.

Una delle grandi sfide di questo progetto è stata quella di riuscire a integrare i vari livelli accanto a una piscina. Di solito, le piscine che sorgono sui tetti degli edifici vengono costruite sopra una base elevata. Un lato di tale piattaforma è stato usato come schienale di un lungo sofà della zona *chill-out*. Al lato opposto, è stato progettato un solarium da cui si accede direttamente alla piscina.

Um dos grandes desafios deste projecto foi o de conjugar os diferentes níveis criados pela colocação da piscina, uma vez que as piscinas construídas no cimo dos edifícios são colocadas sobre uma plataforma elevada. Assim, um dos lados desta plataforma foi aproveitado para encosto de um comprido sofá da zona *chill-out*. No outro lado, foi criado um solário que dá acesso directo à piscina.

En av de stora utmaningarna med det här projektet var att förena de olika nivåskillnaderna intill poolen. Pooler på tak byggs på en upphöjd plattform. Man använde sig av den här plattformens ena sida som ryggstöd för en lång soffa i "chill- out"-utrymmet. På andra sidan skapades en solterass med direkt tillträde till poolen.

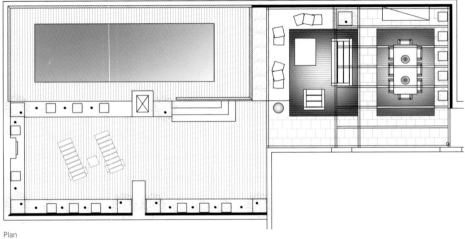

Plan

INSPIRATIONS: ROOF GARDENS

TOITS-JARDINS · DACHGÄRTEN · DAKTERRASSEN · CUBIERTAS AJARDINADAS · GIARDINI PENSILI ·
COBERTURAS AJARDINADAS · TAKTERRASSER

PHOTO CREDITS